HOW TO BE A
Scientist

Written by
Steve Mould

Written by Steve Mould
Consultant Lisa Burke

Senior editor Sam Priddy
Project art editor Joanne Clark
Project editor Allison Singer
US editor Jenny Siklos
Design assistants Molly Lattin,
Bettina Myklebust Stovne
Additional design Emma Hobson,
Katie Knutton, Hoa Luc
Jacket coordinator Francesca Young
Jacket designer Amy Keast
Pre-production producer Dragana Puvacic
Producers Srijana Gurung, Isabell Schart
Managing editor Laura Gilbert
Managing art editor Diane Peyton Jones
Art director Martin Wilson
Publisher Sarah Larter
Publishing director Sophie Mitchell

First American Edition, 2017
Published in the United States by DK Publishing
345 Hudson Street, New York, New York 10014

A catalog record for this book is available
from the Library of Congress.
ISBN: 978-1-4654-6121-6

DK books are available at special discounts when purchased
in bulk for sales promotions, premiums, fund-raising,
or educational use. For details, contact:
DK Publishing Special Markets, 345 Hudson Street,
New York, New York 10014
SpecialSales@dk.com

Printed and bound in China

A WORLD OF IDEAS:
SEE ALL THERE IS TO KNOW

www.dk.com

Contents

How the book works

In *How to be a Scientist*, you will learn how to think and act like a scientist. The book is full of fun activities that can be done at home, as well as simple scientific explanations and a look at some of the most famous scientists of all time.

Awesome activities

These pages feature science projects for you to try yourself. The results you get may not be the same as those in the book—but that's ok! If the results don't match up, try to work out what you did differently, and then try it again.

The science behind each project is explained with the help of diagrams.

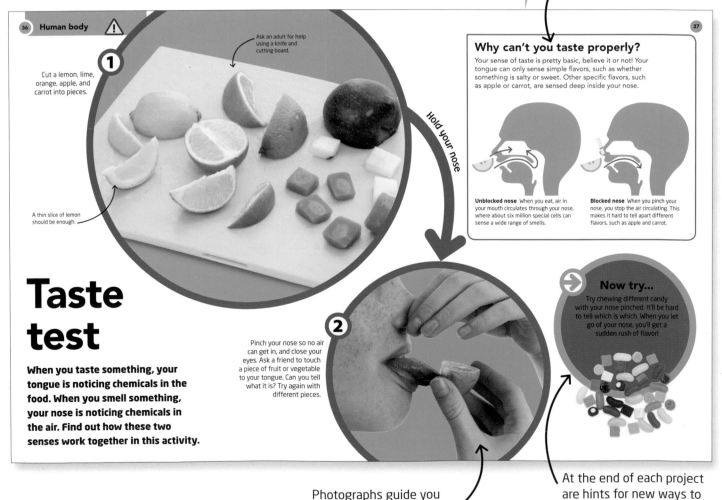

36   Human body

1 Cut a lemon, lime, orange, apple, and carrot into pieces.

Ask an adult for help using a knife and cutting board.

A thin slice of lemon should be enough.

Hold your nose

Taste test

When you taste something, your tongue is noticing chemicals in the food. When you smell something, your nose is noticing chemicals in the air. Find out how these two senses work together in this activity.

2 Pinch your nose so no air can get in, and close your eyes. Ask a friend to touch a piece of fruit or vegetable to your tongue. Can you tell what it is? Try again with different pieces.

37

Why can't you taste properly?

Your sense of taste is pretty basic, believe it or not! Your tongue can only sense simple flavors, such as whether something is salty or sweet. Other specific flavors, such as apple or carrot, are sensed deep inside your nose.

Unblocked nose When you eat, air in your mouth circulates through your nose, where about six million special cells can sense a wide range of smells.

Blocked nose When you pinch your nose, you stop the air circulating. This makes it hard to tell apart different flavors, such as apple and carrot.

Now try...

Try chewing different candy with your nose pinched. It'll be hard to tell which is which. When you let go of your nose, you'll get a sudden rush of flavor!

Photographs guide you through all of the steps.

At the end of each project are hints for new ways to test what you have learned.

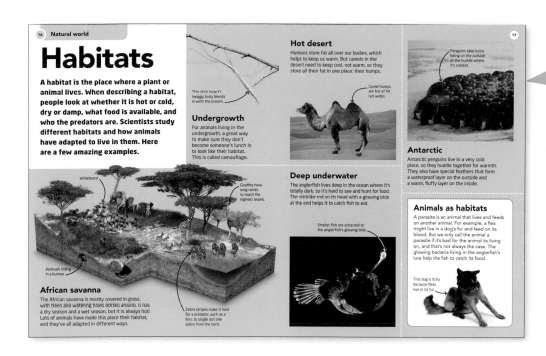

Cool science

The topics on these pages cover everything from habitats and body parts to the Solar System and energy. They will help you to understand the science behind the activities in the book.

Great scientists

The stories behind groundbreaking scientists are brought to life in these pages. Learn about their greatest discoveries, and find out what made them such brilliant scientists in the first place.

Safety first

All of the projects in this book should be done with care. If you see this symbol at the top of a page it means that you will need an adult to help you with the activity below.

Take particular care when:

- you are using sharp objects, such as scissors, knives, or pins
- you are using hot water
- you are near ponds or lakes
- it is dark
- you are lifting anything heavy

Getting ready

Don't forget a pencil or pen so you can make notes!

You can dive right into many of the projects in this book using items you have at home or by exploring outside. There are also a few special tools that you can use to help with your scientific investigations.

If a project calls for cutting something, scissors are essential.

A magnifying glass makes it easier to see small details.

Your tools

Scientists use special equipment to build experiments, to see things they can't normally see, and to measure correctly. Here are some tools that scientists use to help them as they work.

Use a ruler to measure length. It's much more accurate than guessing.

A stopwatch is a good tool for measuring time. You can also use a watch or a clock.

00:02.21

Binoculars will
help you to observe
something far away.

Thinking like a scientist

Equipment can be useful, but being a scientist
isn't about having the right tools—it's about
the way you think. This list of tips will help
you think like a scientist.

1 Scientists are curious. Always ask
questions about how the world works.

2 Scientists are creative. Use your
imagination to come up with explanations
for things. In science, a possible explanation
for something is called a hypothesis.

3 Scientists pay attention. Look for clues that
match your hypothesis—and for clues that
don't match, too!

4 Scientists try to prove themselves wrong.
Once you've got a hypothesis, think of ways
you might show that it isn't true. That's the
best way to test if your idea is right.

5 Scientists share their ideas. Working with
others will help you to come up with new
ideas and find mistakes you wouldn't have
found by yourself.

6 Scientists explore new ideas. Following
the instructions in this book will make the
projects work, but if you try them in a
different way, you may find something
totally new.

7 Scientists have a can-do attitude. Be ready
to take on any challenge, even the ones
that seem tricky. You can do it!

Animals

Habitats

Bacteria

Life

Flowers

Natural world

Scientists are fascinated by life itself, from tiny bacteria to giant blue whales. Whether it's curing diseases or learning how to protect our environment, the science of the natural world has never been so important.

Trees

Evolution

Plants

Environment

Fossils

Collect a few pine cones either from the woods or from a store.

1

Flip one over

2

Look at the bottom of the pine cone. Do you see how the scales form spirals, or curved lines? Count the clockwise spirals, like in the picture above.

Pine cone
patterns

Science is all about finding patterns in the world around you. These patterns are rules that tell us how things will look and behave. They can be easy to spot, but only if you know where to look...

Count in the other direction

Why are the numbers special?

The numbers of spirals you counted should be in this list: 1, 2, 3, 5, 8, 13, 21, 34, 55… In fact the numbers of clockwise and counterclockwise spirals should be next to each other, like 8 and 13. It turns out that arranging spirals in this way packs them together without leaving any gaps. This special list of numbers is called the Fibonacci sequence, and it was discovered by the mathematician Fibonacci in the 12th century.

- Fibonacci
- Born c. 1170
- From Italy

Look around Can you find other plants that have this pattern? If you can't find a pine cone, you may not have to look any further than your kitchen! Try counting the spirals on artichokes or pineapples.

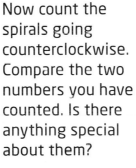

Artichoke

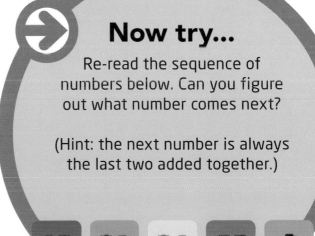

Pineapple

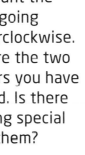

3 Now count the spirals going counterclockwise. Compare the two numbers you have counted. Is there anything special about them?

Now try...

Re-read the sequence of numbers below. Can you figure out what number comes next?

(Hint: the next number is always the last two added together.)

| 13 | 21 | 34 | 55 | ? |

First you need to find a flower, such as this tulip. Ask a grown-up if you can take one from the garden or buy one from a store.

1

Cut it up

2

Carefully use a pair of safety scissors to chop the plant into its different parts.

Lay out the parts

Take it apart

We're always being told to be careful with things and not to break anything. But scientists like to take a different approach—they love taking things apart to see how they work. Let's investigate how this plant works by breaking it into pieces.

3

Lay all of the parts down next to each other and try to name them. What does each part do?

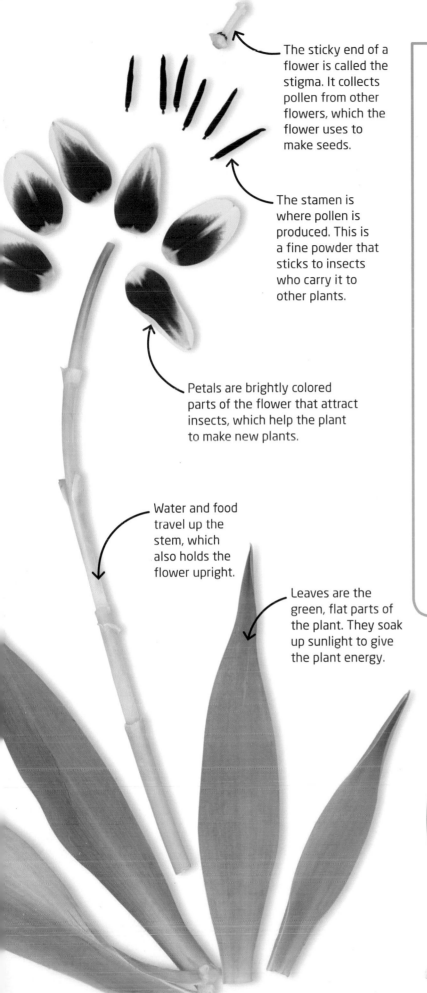

The sticky end of a flower is called the stigma. It collects pollen from other flowers, which the flower uses to make seeds.

The stamen is where pollen is produced. This is a fine powder that sticks to insects who carry it to other plants.

Petals are brightly colored parts of the flower that attract insects, which help the plant to make new plants.

Water and food travel up the stem, which also holds the flower upright.

Leaves are the green, flat parts of the plant. They soak up sunlight to give the plant energy.

Why do we take things apart?

Taking things apart is one way of increasing our understanding of a subject. A lot of what we know about the human body, for example, was discovered by a scientist called Andreas Vesalius. He cut up the dead bodies of criminals to see how all of the various parts were linked.

- Andreas Vesalius
- Born in 1514
- From Belgium

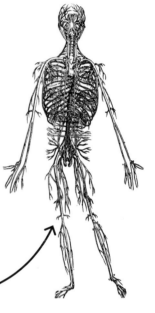

A drawing from Vesalius's famous book on the human body, *De humani corporis fabrica.* The title means "On the fabric of the human body."

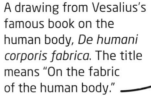

Now try...

Flowers come in all sorts of shapes and sizes, but they all have the same parts. Try taking apart different types of flowers to see for yourself.

Add paper clips

1

To make your own sycamore helicopters, first cut some thick paper or card into different shapes like these.

Try making a variety of sizes from 1 to 2 in (2 to 6 cm) long.

2

Attach the paper clip to this end.

Attach a paper clip to the narrow end of each shape.

Sycamore helicopters

Humans are great inventors, and some of our best ideas come from nature. When an inventor is inspired by something in nature, it is called biomimicry. In this activity about sycamore tree seeds, you will be using a bit of biomimicry, too.

Throw them in the air!

The paper clip adds weight in just the right way to help the helicopter to spin.

Why does it spin?

As a sycamore seed falls, air pushes up against the blade, or the thin part of the seed. The way the blade is curved means the air pushes it sideways, making the seed twirl. This allows the seed to travel a long way from the tree. Where a seed lands, a new tree may begin to grow. If the seeds didn't scatter, they would land on top of one another and wouldn't have room to grow.

3

Throw your sycamore helicopters in the air, or drop them from a great height, and watch them spin down. Which ones work best?

You might need to bend the paper slightly to get the seed to spin well.

Habitats

A habitat is the place where a plant or animal lives. When describing a habitat, people look at whether it is hot or cold, dry or damp, what food is available, and who the predators are. Scientists study different habitats and how animals have adapted to live in them. Here are a few amazing examples.

This stick insect's twiggy body blends in with the branch.

Undergrowth

For animals living in the undergrowth, a great way to make sure they don't become someone's lunch is to look like their habitat. This is called camouflage.

Wildebeest

Giraffes have long necks to reach the highest leaves.

Aardvark hiding in a burrow

Zebra stripes make it hard for a predator, such as a lion, to single out one zebra from the herd.

African savanna

The African savanna is mostly covered in grass, with trees and watering holes dotted around. It has a dry season and a wet season, but it is always hot! Lots of animals have made this place their habitat, and they've all adapted in different ways.

Hot desert

Humans store fat all over our bodies, which helps to keep us warm. But camels in the desert need to keep cool, not warm, so they store all their fat in one place: their humps.

Camel humps are full of fat, not water.

Penguins take turns being on the outside of the huddle where it's coldest.

Antarctic

Antarctic penguins live in a very cold place, so they huddle together for warmth. They also have special feathers that form a waterproof layer on the outside and a warm, fluffy layer on the inside.

Deep underwater

The anglerfish lives deep in the ocean where it's totally dark, so it's hard to see and hunt for food. The sticklike rod on its head with a glowing blob at the end helps it to catch fish to eat.

Smaller fish are attracted to the anglerfish's glowing blob.

Animals as habitats

A parasite is an animal that lives and feeds on another animal. For example, a flea might live in a dog's fur and feed on its blood. But we only call the animal a parasite if it's bad for the animal its living on, and that's not always the case. The glowing bacteria living in the anglerfish's lure help the fish to catch its food.

This dog is itchy because fleas live in its fur.

Bug chambers

Shrimp and crabs belong to a group of animals called crustaceans. Most of them live in the ocean, but believe it or not, pill bugs are crustaceans, too! This experiment shows just how much they love water.

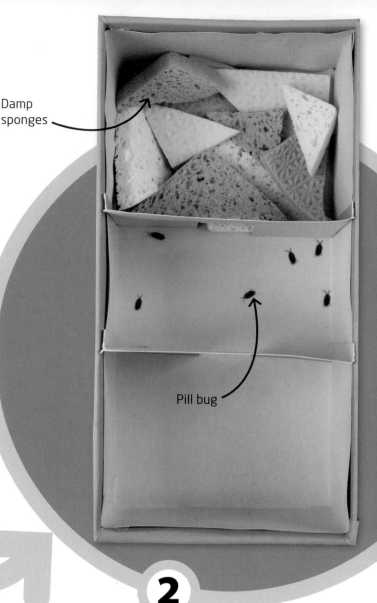

Damp sponges

Pill bug

2

Put a layer of damp sponges in one of the chambers. Collect pill bugs from outdoors, and put them in the middle chamber.

Put in sponges

Make the doorway about 1 in (3 cm) wide and 1 in (3 cm) tall.

Box split into chambers

1

Cut two pieces of cardboard the same width as a shoe box, and cut little doorways in them. Stick them inside the box to make three chambers.

Observing animals

A person who studies animal behavior is called an ethologist. One of the most famous ethologists is Jane Goodall. She discovered lots of amazing things about chimpanzees, such as the fact that they make and use tools. We used to think only humans did that! She also discovered that they tickle and hug each other.

- **Jane Goodall**
- **Born in 1934**
- **From the UK**

Tickling each other is just one of the ways chimpanzees communicate.

Wait 10 minutes

You may need to look under the sponges.

Now try...

Are you sure the pill bugs went to the damp side because it was damp? They may have been trying to hide. Try the experiment again, but this time put dry sponges in the other chamber.

3 After 10 minutes, count the number of pill bugs in each of the chambers. You should find there are more hiding on the damp side. Don't forget to return the pill bugs outdoors when you've finished!

Charles Darwin

Naturalist • Born in 1809 • From the UK

Charles Darwin trained as a doctor, but after leaving college he became fascinated with nature instead. He is famous for his theory of evolution, which is one of the most important scientific ideas of all time. It explains how all of life on Earth—every animal, plant, bacteria, and virus—came to exist.

Darwin's journey

Darwin went on a five-year voyage around the world that showed him that animals aren't the same from one place to another. He was puzzled, until he figured it out—animals in different places had evolved, or adapted to their environment, differently.

Galápagos Islands These South American islands inspired Darwin. There he saw animals that had adapted to each island, such as tortoises on one island that looked different from tortoises on another.

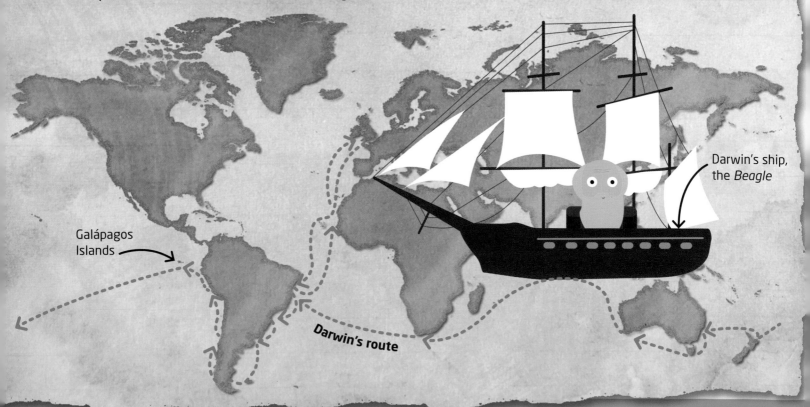

Galápagos Islands

Darwin's ship, the *Beagle*

Darwin's route

What is evolution?

A good example of Darwin's theory of evolution is the marble crayfish. One marble crayfish can reproduce on its own. When it has babies, the babies grow up to be identical to their parent. Sometimes something goes wrong, and one baby isn't a perfect copy. The thing that makes it different is called a mutation. Mutations are usually bad, as they can stop an animal's body from working properly. But they're not *always* bad....

The improved crayfish will survive to have more babies than the original.

Very rarely, a mutation will make the baby better at surviving. This crayfish's slightly different color means it is better hidden from predators.

The marble crayfish makes babies that are identical to it.

The standard crayfish will have a normal number of babies.

Evolution in action

Some insects have "eye spots" like those on this owl butterfly. Looking like an owl helps it avoid being attacked by predators. This means a butterfly with a big eye spot has a better chance at surviving, so the species has evolved to have bigger and clearer eye spots over time.

Eye spot

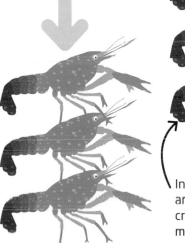

In a competition for food and survival, the standard crayfish will lose to the mutant. The mutant-type crayfish will take over!

Egg roll

Eggs have their particular shape for many reasons. For instance, being round on one end and tapered, or slightly narrower, on the other makes them easier for chickens to lay. Why else is the egg shape so excellent? Let's find out.

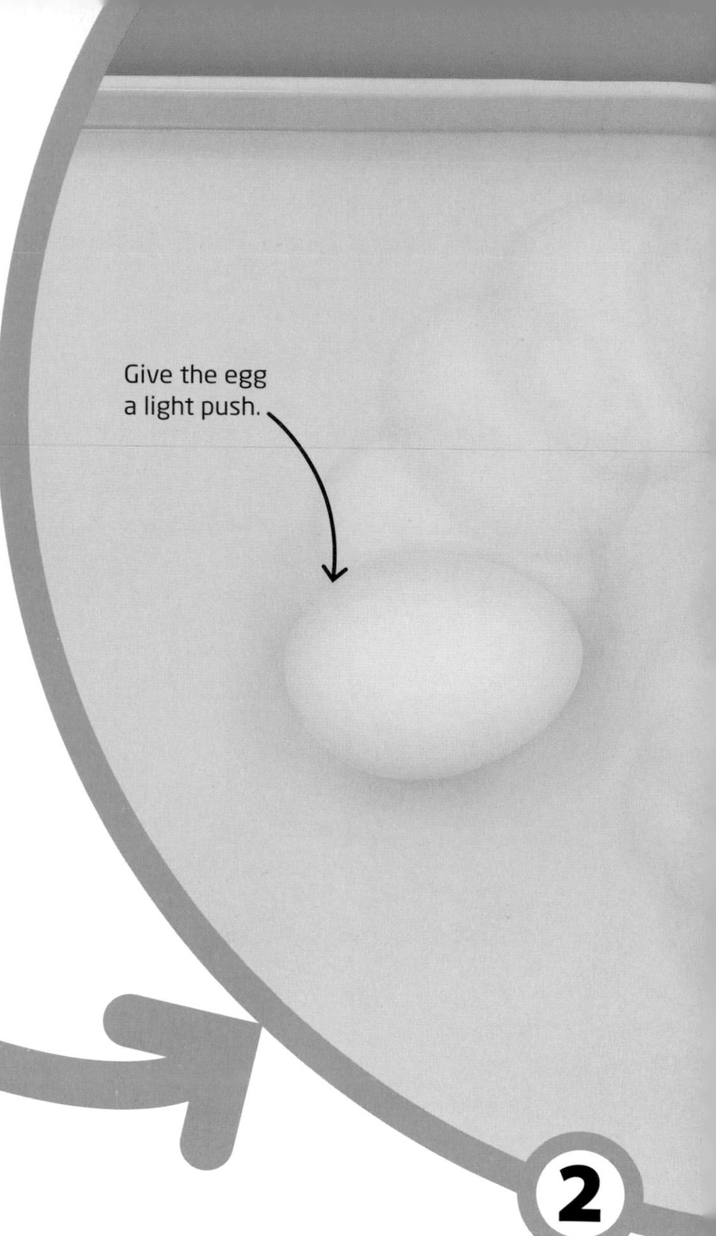

Give the egg a light push.

Try on a level surface

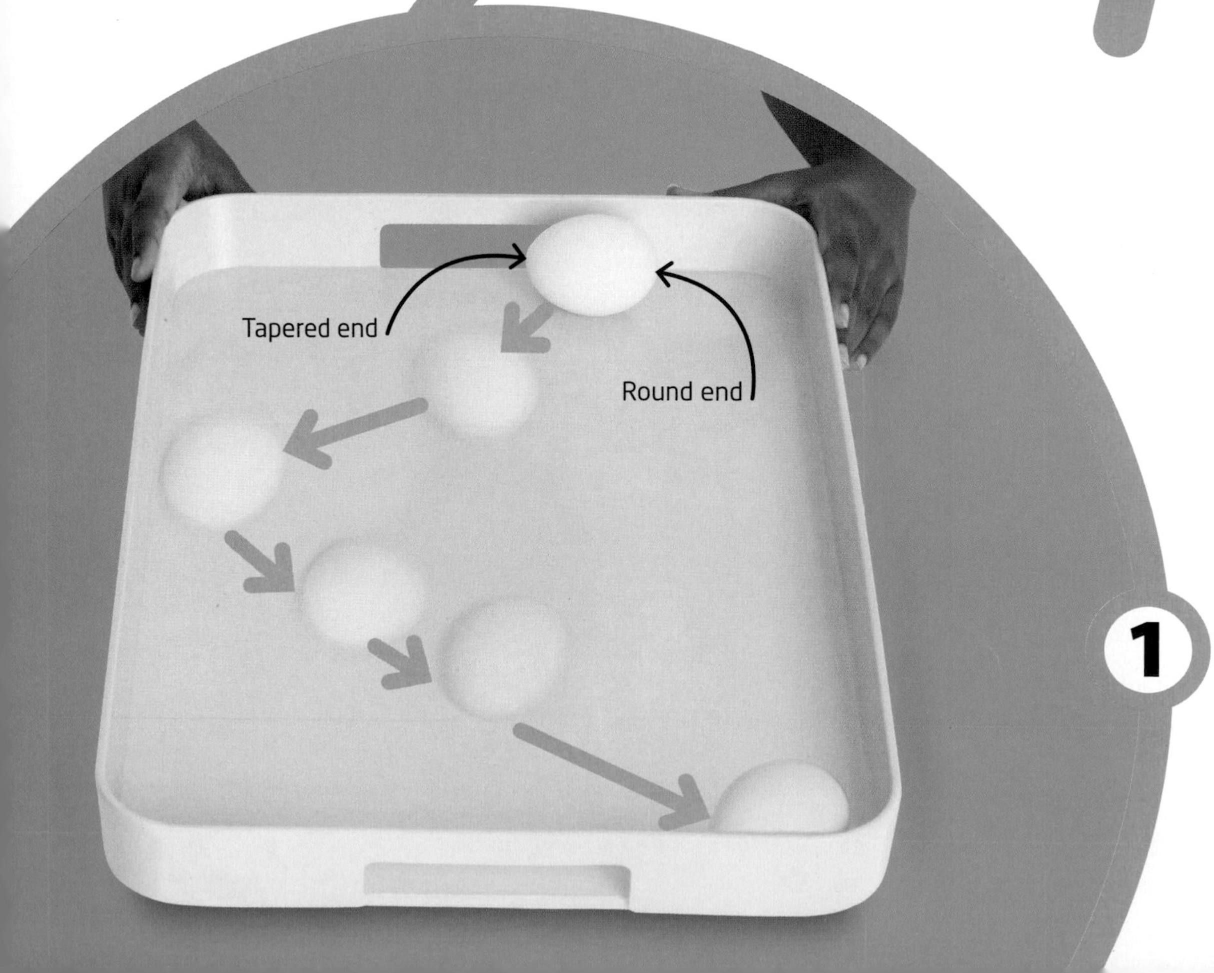

Tapered end

Round end

2 Now lay the tray flat. When you give the egg a nudge, does it roll straight across the tray, or does it roll in a curve?

1 Put an egg on a tray, then tilt the tray. Does the egg roll straight down the tray or go from side to side?

Curved path

Igloos are
extra strong
because of their
dome shape.

Why does shape matter?

The tapered shape of an egg stops it rolling in a straight line from the nest. For birds living on cliff edges, such as the guillemot, this is very important. Scientists believe this is why their eggs are even pointier than most—they evolved to be pointier and pointier over time.

Round eggs If a guillemot egg was completely round, like a ball, it could easily roll off the cliff and break.

Pointy eggs Guillemot eggs are pointy at one end, so they roll in a circle. The pointier the egg, the more tightly it rolls.

Dome strength

Being dome-shaped is also what makes an egg shell so strong. Since there are no corners or angles, any weight put on a dome is supported evenly by the whole structure. That's why engineers often use domes when designing roofs and bridges.

Mary Anning

Palaeontologist • Born in 1799 • From the UK

Mary Anning came from a poor family. She figured out how to find amazing fossils, which are ancient animals or plants preserved in rock, and made money selling them. Some of her finds were 200 million years old, from the time of the dinosaurs! Now she is celebrated as a great fossil hunter who changed the way we see the world.

Fossil hunting

Anning made many important finds, including two ancient sea reptiles—the ichthyosaur and the plesiosaur. She also dug up amazing fossilized shells. People didn't believe there had been creatures living a long time ago that no longer existed, but Anning's discoveries proved otherwise.

Coprolite Anning's discoveries showed that a mysterious type of rock, now called coprolite, was actually fossilized poop.

Lyme Regis Most of Anning's fossil hunting took place where she lived—on the fossil-rich coast around Lyme Regis in the United Kingdom.

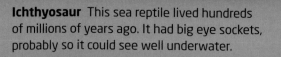

Ichthyosaur This sea reptile lived hundreds of millions of years ago. It had big eye sockets, probably so it could see well underwater.

Recording findings

Anning read as many academic papers as she could find, sometimes copying them by hand and adding detailed notes. On the right is the letter she wrote announcing her discovery of the plesiosaur, along with her detailed drawing.

Charles Darwin link

Geologist Adam Sedgwick bought many fossils from Anning. He taught geology to Charles Darwin at the University of Cambridge. Darwin may have been able to see and study some of Anning's fossils, helping him to develop his theory of evolution.

No women allowed!

The Geological Society of London didn't allow Anning in because she was a woman. She also didn't always get credit for her findings. People today realize and appreciate just how important her discoveries really were.

Ammonite shell This shell was Anning's most common find. It's the shell of a mollusk whose closest living relatives include the octopus, squid, and cuttlefish.

Plesiosaur The plesiosaur was the largest sea-dwelling reptile when it lived on Earth more than 205 million years ago.

Food chains

A food chain links plants and animals according to who eats what. They help us to see how different living things in an environment depend on eating one another for survival. Food chains are one of the tools scientists use to describe the world around them.

Rabbit

Animals like this rabbit that eat producers are called primary consumers. Rabbits are herbivores, which means they eat plants in order to get the energy and nutrients they need for survival.

Grass

Plants, like grass, are at the bottom of the food chain. They use energy from the Sun and nutrients from the soil to make, or produce, their own food. That's why we call them producers.

Snake

Animals that eat primary consumers are called secondary consumers. This snake eats rabbits. Its digestive system (the part of its body that breaks down food) takes in energy and nutrients from meat.

Eagle

Animals at the top of a food chain, like this eagle, are called apex predators. Nothing hunts or eats an apex predator, so the food chain ends here. Other apex predators include polar bears, killer whales, and African lions.

Decomposers

Bacteria that feed on dead animals are called decomposers. Other decomposers include some worms, like the earthworms in this picture, and fungi. When an eagle or other apex predator dies, decomposers feed on its meat and recycle nutrients back into the soil for plants to use. Then the cycle begins again!

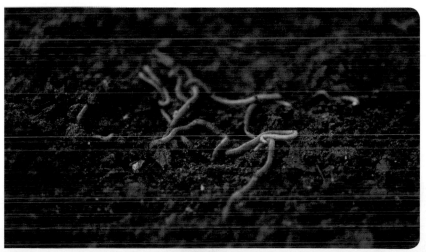

Pond life

Ponds are absolutely full of life. In fact a teaspoon full of pond water contains millions of bacteria. Bacteria can't be seen without a microscope, but if you look close enough, you will be able to see some of the bigger creatures.

Fill up a jar with water

1

Find a jar with a lid that screws on, and go with an adult to a nearby pond. Carefully scoop out a jar full of water. Make sure to put the lid on securely so it doesn't spill.

What do you see?

If you see things that are about ⅛ in (1 to 5 mm) long swimming around in short bursts, they're probably daphnia. Daphnia are tiny animals that live in ponds and lakes. There's a chance you'll also see a daphnia being eaten by a hydra. Hydra are animals that look like little tubes. You can find them hanging on to plant matter.

Taking notes
Don't forget to write down or draw what you see.

Daphnia

Use a magnifying glass to look even closer.

2

Look closely at the water in the jar. Can you see anything swimming around in there?

Now try...

Look at the daphnia under a microscope if you have one. Daphnia are a little bit see-through, so you can see their organs and even watch their heart beat if you look closely enough.

Making mold

When food goes moldy we tend to get rid of it. But scientists like to study mold and all of its fascinating features. In this experiment, you can grow and study some mold of your own.

Fridge jar   **Windowsill jar**

2

After a week, compare the two jars. Do you see any mold? If so, which jar has more? Write down or draw your findings.

Leave for a week

Make sure the lids are on tight.

Ask an adult to help cut up the fruit into pieces.

1

Cut up different fruits and fill two jars with the pieces. Close the lids. Put one jar in the fridge and the other on a sunny windowsill.

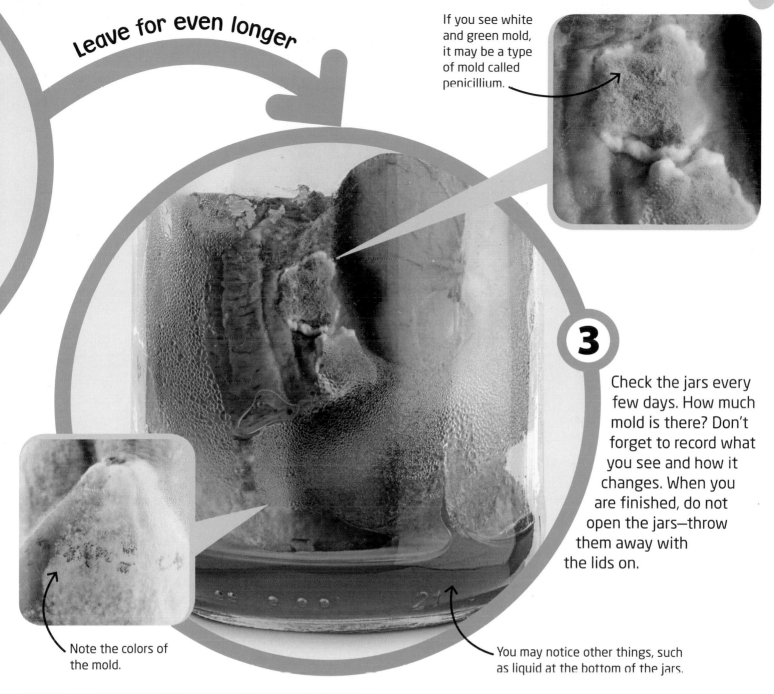

Leave for even longer

If you see white and green mold, it may be a type of mold called penicillium.

3 Check the jars every few days. How much mold is there? Don't forget to record what you see and how it changes. When you are finished, do not open the jars—throw them away with the lids on.

Note the colors of the mold.

You may notice other things, such as liquid at the bottom of the jars.

Why does mold grow?

Mold is a type of fungus, and it makes tiny things called spores that scatter like seeds. Spores are too small to see, but they are floating in the air around you. There were either spores on the fruit or inside the jars before you put on the lids. Mold could then grow because it had food. Because mold loves to grow where it's warm, the fridge helps to slow down growth.

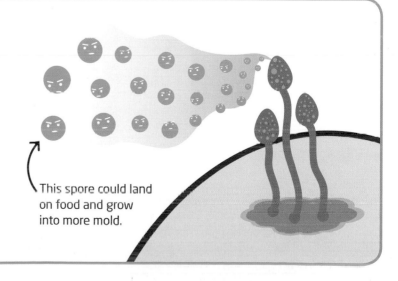

This spore could land on food and grow into more mold.

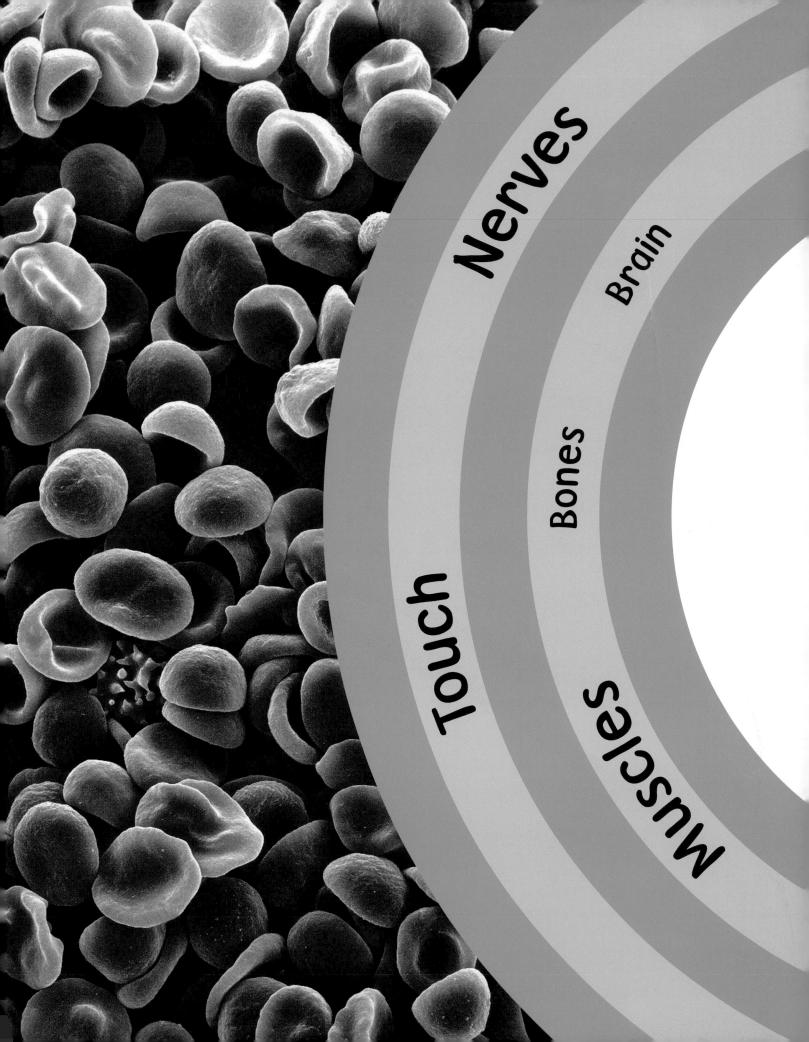

Nerves

Touch

Brain

Bones

Muscles

Human body

The human body is full of surprises, from the way our organs keep us alive to how our senses tell us about the world. Scientists still have much to learn about the mysterious workings of our amazing bodies.

Senses

Smell

Organs

Skin

Blood

Taste

Cells

Body parts

Over 2,000 years ago, scientists in Ancient Greece cut apart human bodies. They looked at the internal organs, such as the lungs and heart, and tried to figure out what each one did. Since then, we've learned a lot about how and why our bodies work the way they do.

What's inside you?

Different organs inside your body combine to make one amazing human body machine. Here are a few of the hardest workers.

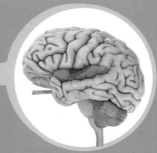

Brain The brain acts like a computer that controls your body. This is where thinking happens.

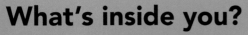

Lungs This organ takes in oxygen from the air we breathe. Our bodies need oxygen to make energy.

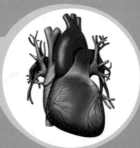

Heart This muscle pumps blood around your body through veins and arteries. It's always working and never gets a cramp!

Liver The liver makes chemicals needed to break down food in a process called digestion.

Stomach Your stomach is full of acids that help break down food into nutrients, which your body needs to stay healthy.

Intestines These long tubes are connected to the stomach. They absorb nutrients, such as vitamins, and water from food.

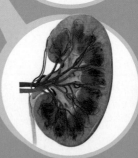

Kidneys This pair of organs keeps the saltiness and acidity of your body at just the right levels. They also make pee.

Skeleton

You'd be just a wobbly sack of organs if it wasn't for your bones. These hard organs join together into a skeleton, which gives your body structure.

Your ribcage protects the organs underneath, such as your heart and lungs. It also rises and widens to pull air into your lungs.

This is the femur, the longest bone in your body. (The smallest bone is in your ear!)

Three bones meet to form your knee: your femur, tibia (shinbone), and patella (kneecap).

Each foot contains 26 bones.

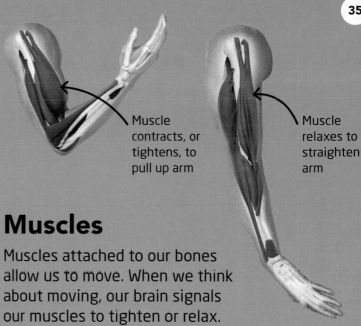

Muscle contracts, or tightens, to pull up arm

Muscle relaxes to straighten arm

Muscles

Muscles attached to our bones allow us to move. When we think about moving, our brain signals our muscles to tighten or relax.

Blood

Blood carries important chemicals around your body and protects you from infection.

Red blood cells carry oxygen.

White blood cells attack bugs and fight off infection.

Blood cells and nutrients are carried around the body in a watery fluid called plasma.

Skin

Your skin is your largest organ. It's about eight times heavier than your brain! Skin is a waterproof layer that protects you from the outside world.

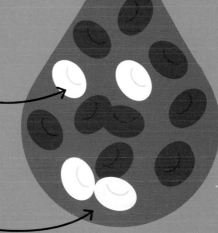

When you get too hot, sweat cools you down.

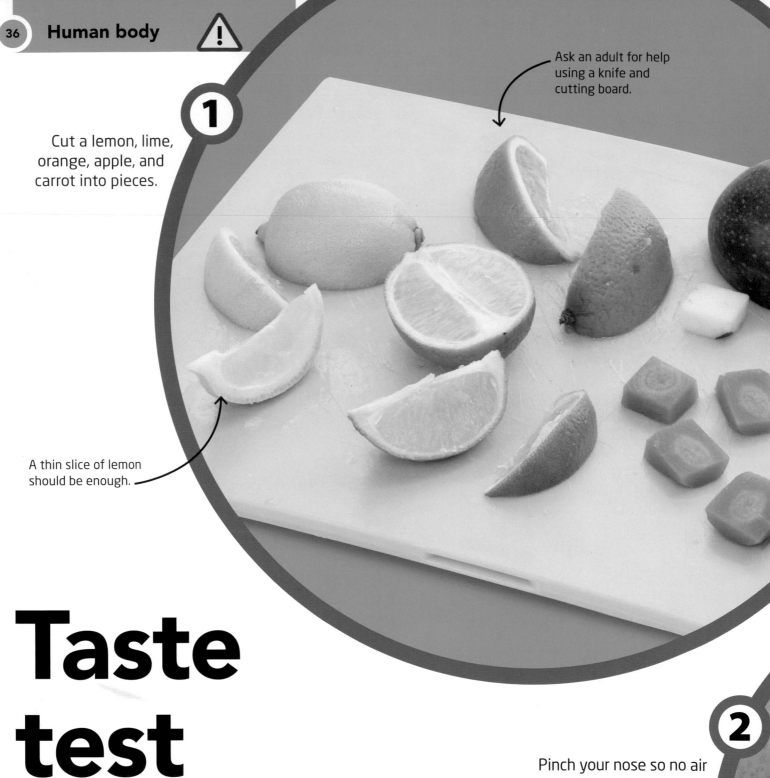

1

Cut a lemon, lime, orange, apple, and carrot into pieces.

Ask an adult for help using a knife and cutting board.

A thin slice of lemon should be enough.

Taste test

When you taste something, your tongue is noticing chemicals in the food. When you smell something, your nose is noticing chemicals in the air. Find out how these two senses work together in this activity.

2

Pinch your nose so no air can get in, and close your eyes. Ask a friend to touch a piece of fruit or vegetable to your tongue. Can you tell what it is? Try again with different pieces.

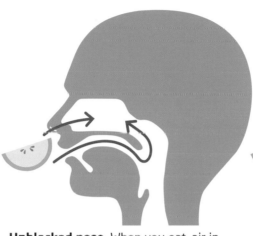

Why can't you taste properly?

Your sense of taste is pretty basic, believe it or not! Your tongue can only sense simple flavors, such as whether something is salty or sweet. Other specific flavors, such as apple or carrot, are sensed deep inside your nose.

Hold your nose

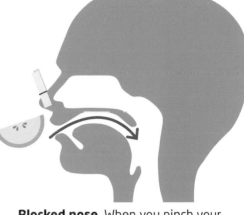

Unblocked nose When you eat, air in your mouth circulates through your nose, where about six million special cells can sense a wide range of smells.

Blocked nose When you pinch your nose, you stop the air circulating. This makes it hard to tell apart different flavors, such as apple and carrot.

Now try...

Try chewing different candy with your nose pinched. It'll be hard to tell which is which. When you let go of your nose, you'll get a sudden rush of flavor!

start rubbing

Lay out a smooth plastic tray, a piece of paper, and a bit of carpet.

1

Use any carpet you have in your house.

Smooth tray

Rough carpet

2

Rub the tray with your left hand and rub the carpet with your right hand at the same time for 30 seconds.

Fool your fingers

Our sense of touch works in strange ways. We may not notice it in our everyday lives, but in science, it's important to dig deeper. This experiment may seem simple, but it uncovers just how complicated your sense of touch can be.

How does it work?

After repeating the same action for enough time, your right hand gets used to the carpet's roughness, so when you switch to paper, the paper feels really smooth. This works with your sense of hearing, too. People who move near noisy airports find it hard to sleep at night at first. However, after a few days they get used to the noise and can sleep more easily.

After 30 seconds...

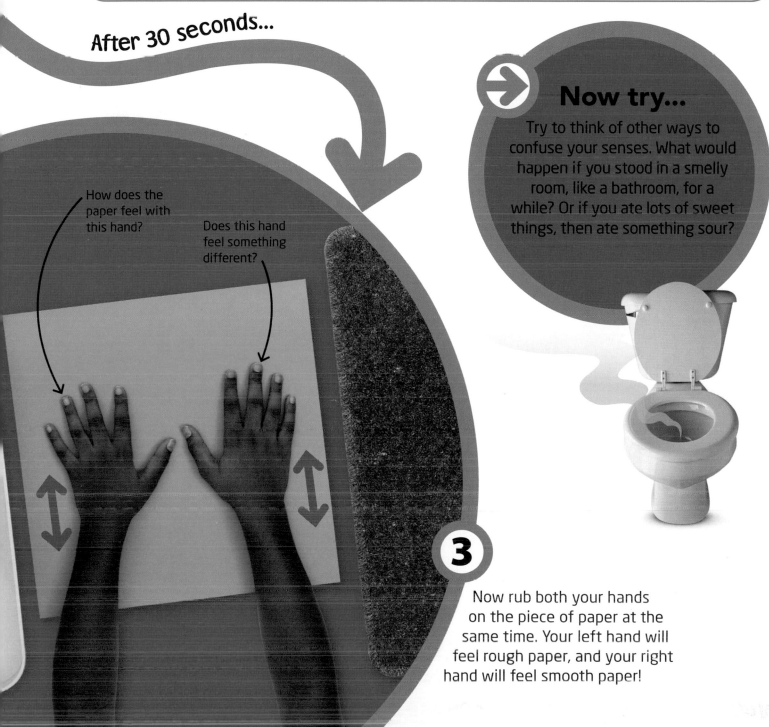

How does the paper feel with this hand?

Does this hand feel something different?

Now try...

Try to think of other ways to confuse your senses. What would happen if you stood in a smelly room, like a bathroom, for a while? Or if you ate lots of sweet things, then ate something sour?

3

Now rub both your hands on the piece of paper at the same time. Your left hand will feel rough paper, and your right hand will feel smooth paper!

Let go

The 0 mark should be level with the top of your friend's hand.

1

Hold a ruler so it hangs between your friend's open thumb and finger.

2

Tell your friend that when you let go of the ruler, it's their job to catch it as fast as possible. Once they understand, wait a few seconds, and then without warning them, let go!

Catch the ruler

Reaction
challenge

Experiments don't always give the same result when you repeat them. That's why scientists do an experiment over and over. They then figure out the average of all the results to come up with a single answer. Can you beat your friend's average reaction time?

How quick were you?

Add up your friend's results, then divide by three. This is your friend's average. Use one of these tables to find their reaction time. Do the same for your results. Who was faster? The lower the reaction time the better! Reaction time is a combination of how long it takes your brain to decide to pinch your fingers and how long it takes the brain signals to travel down your arm.

Centimeters	Reaction time in seconds	Inches	Reaction time in seconds
5	0.10	1	0.07
6	0.11	2	0.10
7	0.12	3	0.12
8	0.13	4	0.14
9	0.14	5	0.16
10	0.14	6	0.18
11	0.15	7	0.19
12	0.16	8	0.20
13	0.16	9	0.22
14	0.17	10	0.23
15	0.17	11	0.24
16	0.18	12	0.25
17	0.19		
18	0.19		
19	0.20		
20	0.20		

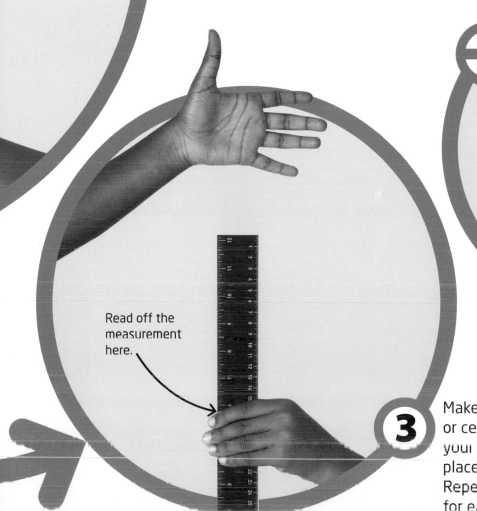

Read off the measurement here.

Now try...

Test your parents, grandparents, or another grown-up. They may not be as good as you! Reaction time often gets slower with age.

3 Make a note of the number of inches or centimeters on the ruler where your friend caught it. Then switch places to get your reaction time. Repeat the experiment three times for each person.

Test your nerves

Our sense of touch is amazing. Put your hand in a backpack and you can tell what most things are without even looking. But how good is your sense of touch on the rest of your body? Find out with this clever test.

2 Ask your friend to close their eyes. With the straws about ½ in (1 cm) apart, press them into your friend's hand and ask them to guess how many straws there are.

Don't poke too hard!

Get poking

1 For this experiment you will need a friend. Pick a number between one and three, and put that many straws in your hand.

3 You'll find that they probably guessed correctly. Ask your friend to turn around and poke a different number of straws into their back. Did they get it right this time?

Why was it easier the first time?

We can sense when something is touching our skin because of nerve endings that lie just under the surface. But not all parts of our body have the same number of nerve endings. Our hands have loads of them tightly packed together, but our backs have hardly any. This means it's much easier to count the straws when they're touching our hands.

Sensitive regions This diagram shows how sensitive different parts of the body are. The bigger the body part on the diagram, the more sensitive it is.

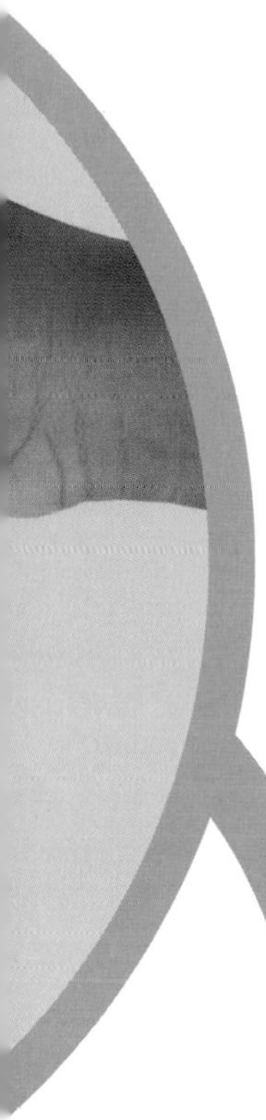

Mix it up

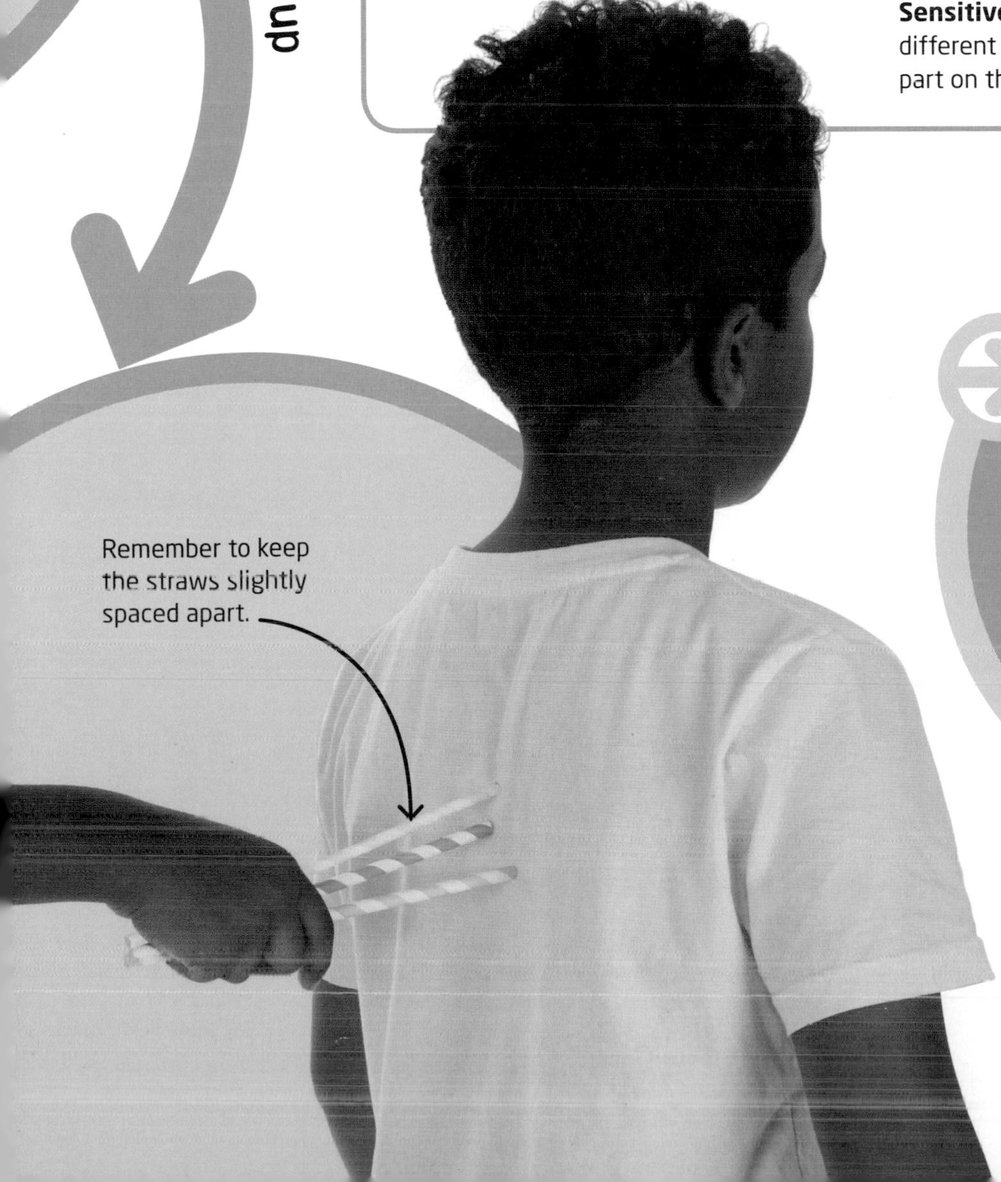

Remember to keep the straws slightly spaced apart.

Now try...

Press a tennis ball into your friend's hand and then their back. Can they identify the object? What other objects could you test?

Rhazes

Biologist and chemist • Born c. 865 • From Iran

Rhazes was a great scientific thinker from the Middle East during a time called the Islamic Golden Age. Many scientists back then were polymaths, meaning they were interested in everything—from math to philosophy. Rhazes's biggest discoveries were in the fields of medicine and biology, which is the study of living things.

Rhazes working in his laboratory

Golden Age

For about 400 years, Baghdad, in present-day Iraq, was the intellectual capital of the world. Rhazes and other Arab thinkers who worked in the city made advances in medicine, created great art and architecture, and invented new math concepts.

Challenging Galen

Rhazes studied the existing medical wisdom of the time, which had been presented 600 years earlier by a Greek physician named Galen. In many cases, Rhazes found Galen to be wrong.

Galen

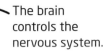

The brain controls the nervous system.

The nerves bundle together in the spinal column before reaching the brain.

The sciatic nerve is the longest nerve in the body.

Control experiment

Rhazes invented the control experiment. This is the idea that if you're testing a new medicine on patients, you should have "control" patients who don't take the medicine. This helps scientists to make sure the medicine's effects aren't just a coincidence.

Patients who have taken the medicine

Patients who have not taken the medicine

If scientists see the same result in both groups, they know it's not an effect of the medicine.

Nervous system

Rhazes was the first person to properly describe what nerves do. He realized that muscles were controlled by nerves connected to the brain. Our senses, such as touch and sight, use this system to send signals back to the brain.

Rhazes was in charge of three hospitals in Iraq and Iran.

Funny faces

Our brains have a special talent for recognizing faces. We have no trouble telling two similar faces apart. We're also good at recognizing facial expressions to tell how someone is feeling. Here's an illusion that messes with your face-recognizing powers.

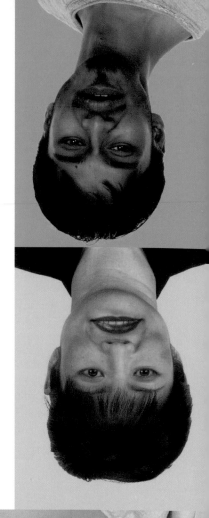

1

Without turning the page or tilting your head, look at these upside-down faces. Can you spot anything strange about them?

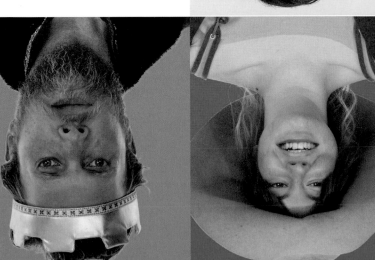

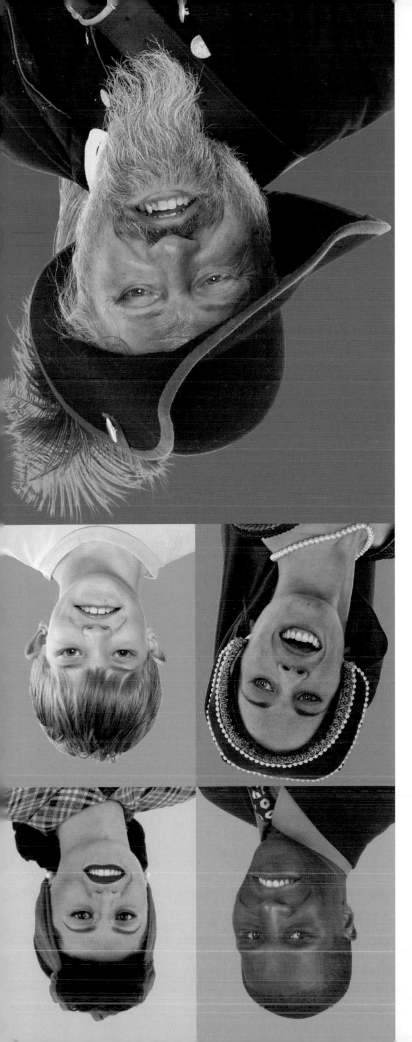

2

Now turn the page and look again. You'll notice very quickly that something is wrong. The mouth and eyes have been turned upside down! But before you turned the page it was very hard to spot. This illusion is called the Thatcher effect.

Recognizing faces

We don't actually know for sure how this illusion works, but we know it's to do with our brain's ability to recognize faces. The part of the brain that helps us to recognize faces is so sensitive that we can't help but see faces all over the place—including in things that aren't alive! Can you spot the faces below?

What do you see?

The way eyesight works in humans is amazing. Special cells at the back of your eyes detect an image, and send electrical signals to the brain. But the way these cells work can be quite strange, as this test will show.

1 Make sure this book is really well lit by sitting under a bright light or going outside. Both of the images above have a small black dot in the middle. Make sure you have found both dots.

2 Stare at the dot in the first image for 30 seconds, then stare at the dot in the second image. The second image is black and white but it should appear in color for a few seconds!

Why do the colors change?

Every color has an opposite, and they can all be arranged in a wheel. When you stare at the dot, the image on the back of your eye stays still. This makes the special cells in your eye less sensitive to the colors in the image, and so you notice the opposite colors in the color wheel more. This means that if you stare at something blue, then anything you look at afterward will seem less blue, or in other words more yellow!

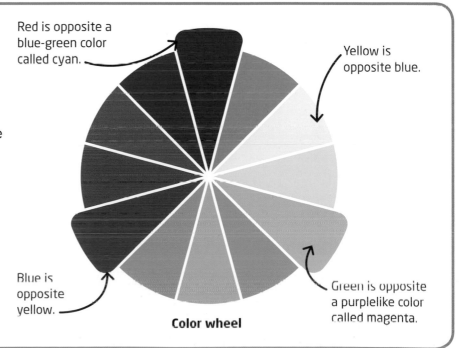

Red is opposite a blue-green color called cyan.

Yellow is opposite blue.

Blue is opposite yellow.

Green is opposite a purplelike color called magenta.

Color wheel

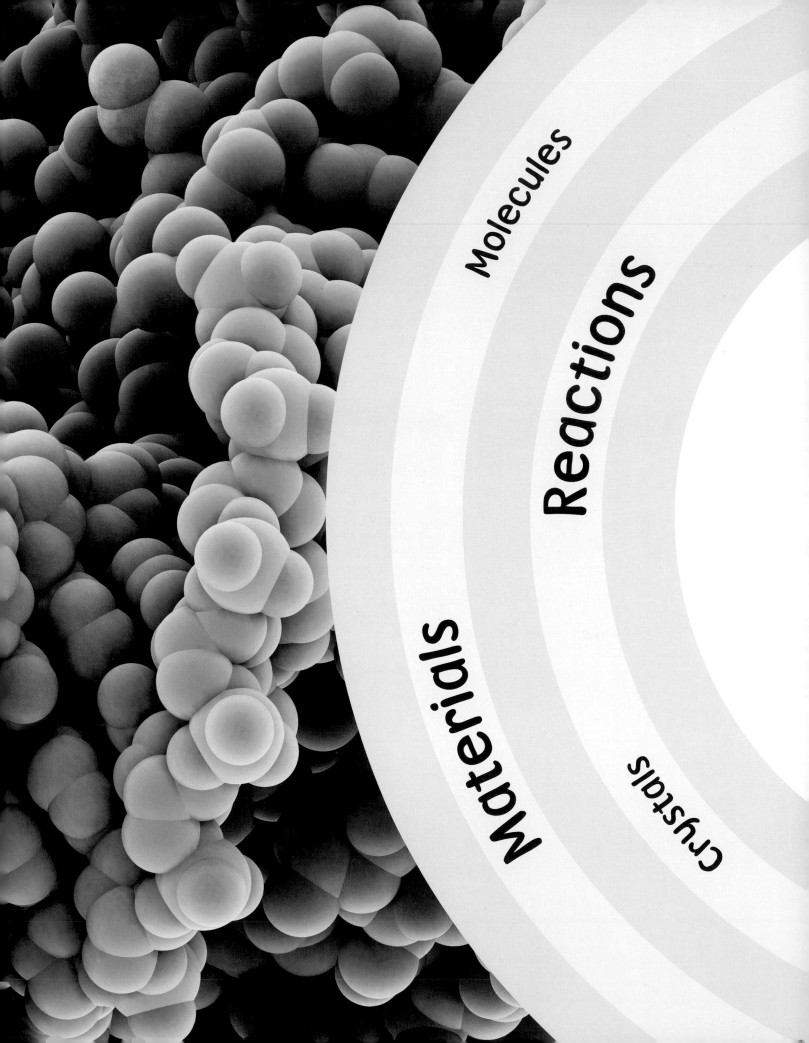

Molecules

Reactions

Materials

Crystals

Atoms

Periodic table

Chemistry

Chemistry is all about combining things in different ways. That's how scientists make new chemicals, and how they come to understand the ones in the world around us. When you mix two totally different things together, the results may surprise you!

Radioactivity

Temperature

What is a chemical?

Everything you can see and touch is made of atoms—tiny ball-like particles that stick together. There are 118 kinds of atoms, and they all have their own special features and abilities. When certain atoms stick together in certain ways, the result is called a chemical.

Chemical make-up

Scientists who study chemistry try to figure out the different ways atoms can stick together to form groups. It's a lot like playing with toy bricks—so many different things can be built with only a few pieces. On these pages you will discover the chemistry behind everyday objects.

Plastic When atoms stick together in a chain tens of thousands of atoms long, it's called a polymer. Plastic is an example of a polymer. This toy is made of a plastic called PVC.

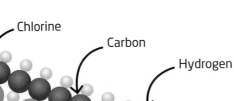

Chlorine

Carbon

Hydrogen

Water Two hydrogen atoms stuck to an oxygen atom makes a molecule of water. A water molecule is much smaller than a polymer molecule.

Hydrogen

Oxygen

Chemical reactions

When you burn wood, you change the way the atoms are arranged. Carbon and hydrogen atoms break apart and stick to oxygen atoms in the air. When atoms are rearranged like this, it's called a chemical reaction.

Inside an atom

Atoms are unimaginably small. There are about 100 trillion in the period at the end of this sentence. Each atom is made of smaller particles called protons, neutrons, and electrons.

The center of the atom is called the nucleus. It is made of protons (red) and neutrons (green).

Electrons are positioned in a fuzzy cloud around the nucleus.

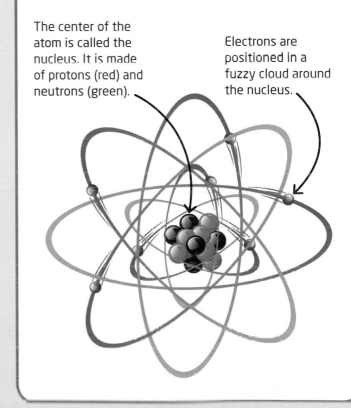

Salt If you stick loads of sodium and chlorine atoms together, you get a crystal of salt. Unlike a molecule, a crystal can vary in size.

Sodium

Chlorine

Dmitri Mendeleev

Chemist • Born in 1834 • From Russia

Atoms are the building blocks of everything you see around you. Dmitri Mendeleev is famous because he made a list of all the different types of atoms, called elements. He arranged them all in a grid called the periodic table.

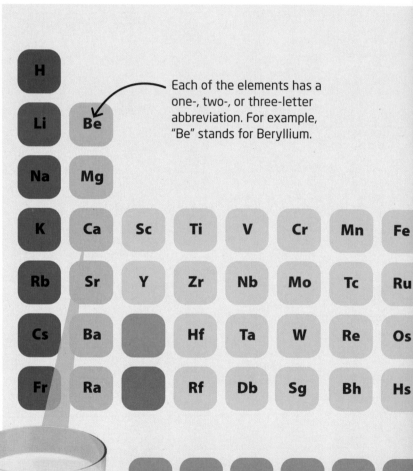

Each of the elements has a one-, two-, or three-letter abbreviation. For example, "Be" stands for Beryllium.

The periodic table

When Mendeleev put the elements in order by weight, he saw patterns. For example, helium doesn't like sticking to other atoms, and when you go forward eight elements, there's another element that behaves the same way—neon. He listed the elements in rows so similar elements line up above and below one another in columns. This is the periodic table.

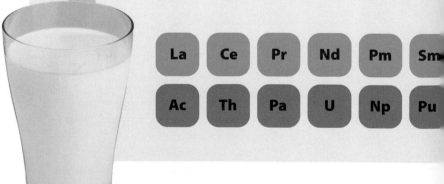

Calcium Calcium helps to build strong bones and is found in milk. It's a shiny metal like the other elements in its column.

Dmitri

Big family

Mendeleev was the youngest of at least 11 brothers and sisters—and maybe as many as 17! After his siblings grew up and left home, Dmitri traveled with his mother all the way across Russia to St. Petersburg in search of a good education.

Gold Gold is a metal used in jewelry. It doesn't corrode, or wear away, easily, just like the other elements in its column.

							He
		B	C	N	O	F	Ne
		Al	Si	P	S	Cl	Ar
Co	Ni	Cu	Zn	Ga	Ge	As	Se	Br	Kr
Rh	Pd	Ag	Cd	In			Te	I	Xe
Ir	Pt	Au	Hg					At	Rn
Mt	Ds		Cn						Uuo

Eu	Gd
Am	Cm

Crystal ball

Mendeleev designed the periodic table with gaps in it. He predicted that each gap was for an element that hadn't yet been discovered. Every time a new element was found in the future, he was proved right!

Cleaning coins

Pull some coins out of your pocket. The ones that appear old have been going through a change that makes them look dull. This kind of change is called a chemical reaction. If you want them to look shiny and new again, you can fight back with a chemical reaction of your own!

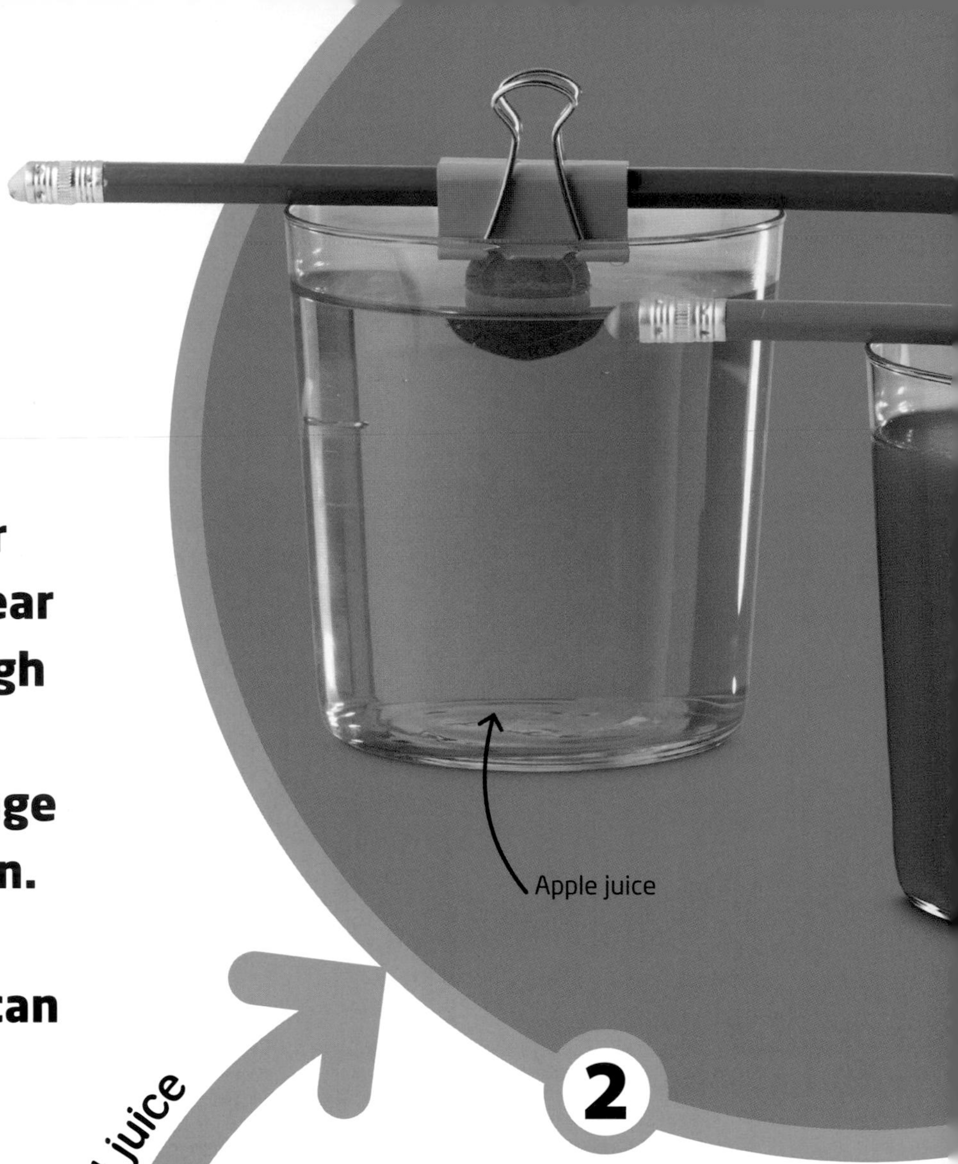

Apple juice

Add juice

2

Add fruit juice until half the coin is covered. You can try different fruit juices to see which one works best.

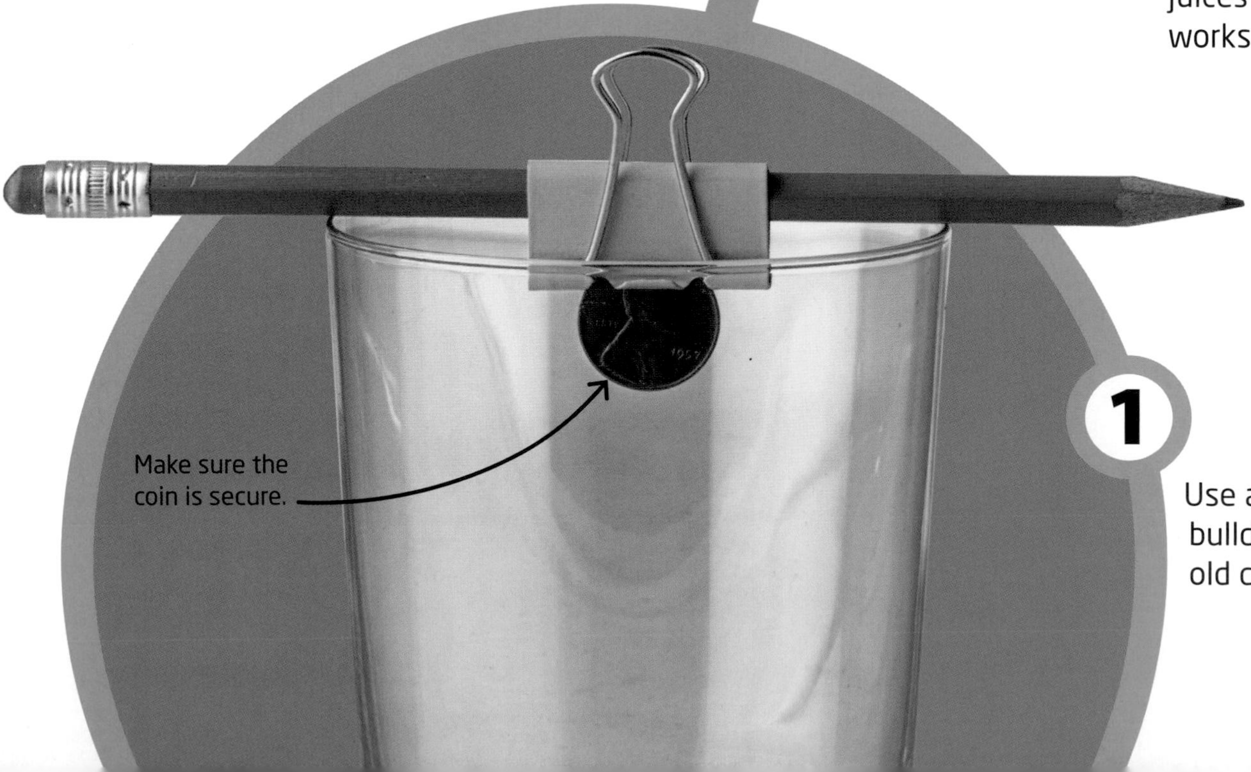

Make sure the coin is secure.

1

Use a pencil and a bulldog clip to hang an old coin over a glass.

Tomato juice

Dirty and dull

Shiny and clean

Wait a while

3

After 30 minutes, remove the coins and give them a rinse in water. The bottom half will be a lot cleaner! Remember to get rid of the juice after finishing the experiment.

Dissolving acids

When coins start to look old, it's because the copper metal is reacting with oxygen in the air to form a layer of copper oxide. Fortunately weak acids, like the citric acid in fruit juice, dissolve the copper oxide.

Copper oxide layer

Citric acid reacts with copper oxide, removing it from the coin.

Now try...

What other liquids will clean a coin? Ketchup? Vinegar? Even cola and other sodas are very weak acids. You might have to leave them overnight to work.

Soda

Ketchup

Vinegar

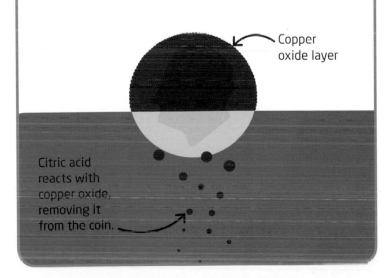

Is black ink really black?

Scientists love to pull things apart and figure out what they're made of. But the really curious ones invent ways to separate things you wouldn't even think to separate—such as black ink!

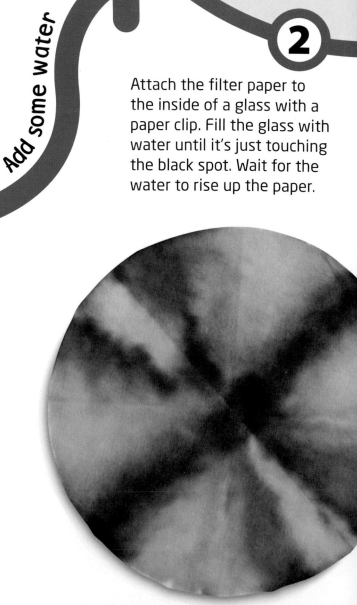

Add some water

2

Attach the filter paper to the inside of a glass with a paper clip. Fill the glass with water until it's just touching the black spot. Wait for the water to rise up the paper.

1

Use a pen to draw a big black dot in the middle of some coffee filter paper. Fold the paper into eighths.

Water comes
up to the
black spot.

Unfold and let dry

What's ink made of?

To get the color just right, pen makers use a mixture of different colored inks. Some of these inks mix into water more easily than others. This means they're more soluble. When the water rises up through the paper, it carries the ink with it. The more soluble ink is carried farther, so all of the different colors are separated on the paper.

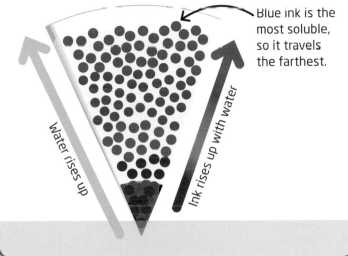

Blue ink is the most soluble, so it travels the farthest.

Water rises up

Ink rises up with water

3 Unfold the paper and look at the colors. You should see a few different colors besides black.

Now try...

Use different types of pen, such as felt tip, ballpoint, whiteboard, and permanent marker. Which pen's ink separates into the most colors? You can also try using different color pens. What happens now?

Make a rainbow

Many people say you shouldn't play with your food, but scientists disagree. Scientists play with all sorts of materials, including food, and make amazing discoveries along the way. Here's an activity to get you started.

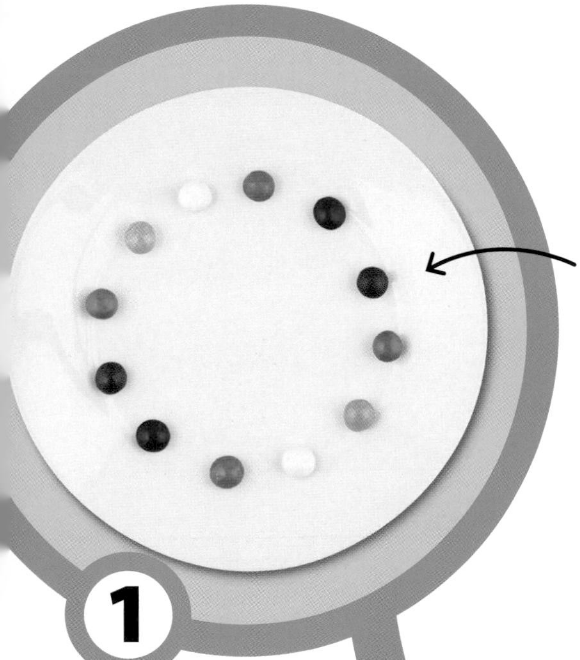

1

Arrange some colored candies in a circle on a plate.

A white plate will work best.

Add water

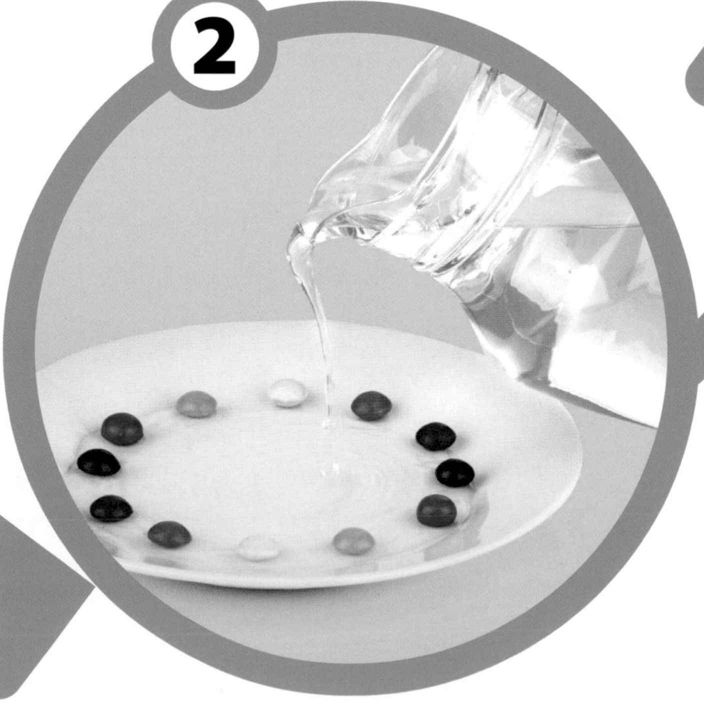

2

Pour a thin layer of water onto the plate. Be careful not to bump the plate and move the candies.

Watch and wait

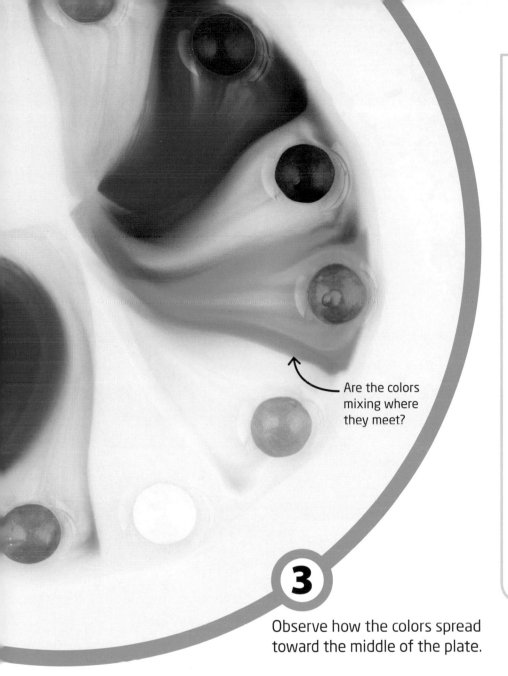

Are the colors mixing where they meet?

3

Observe how the colors spread toward the middle of the plate.

Cup of tea

When you make a cup of tea using a teabag, you don't have to stir or mix the water. The flavors diffuse, or spread out, from the tea leaves into the water—just like the colors from the candies in this experiment.

Why do the colors spread?

Candies get their color from food dye, and food dye dissolves in, or mixes into, water. As the water molecules jiggle around, they spread the dye out. This is called diffusion. All of the colors spread out at the same time, forming stripes that look like a rainbow. If you leave the plate long enough, you will see the different colors start to mix.

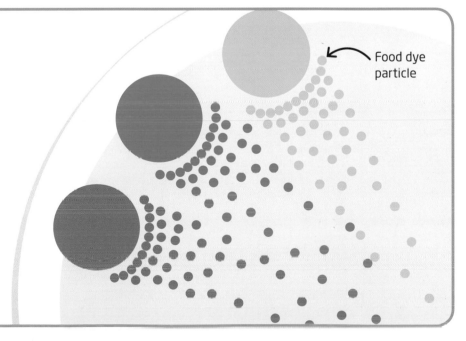

Food dye particle

Materials

We rely on lots of materials in our everyday lives. These materials all have different qualities, such as hardness, softness, and flexibility. These qualities all have their uses. For example, you need a strong, hard material to make a table. Chemists are very interested in exploring exactly why a material has the special qualities it does.

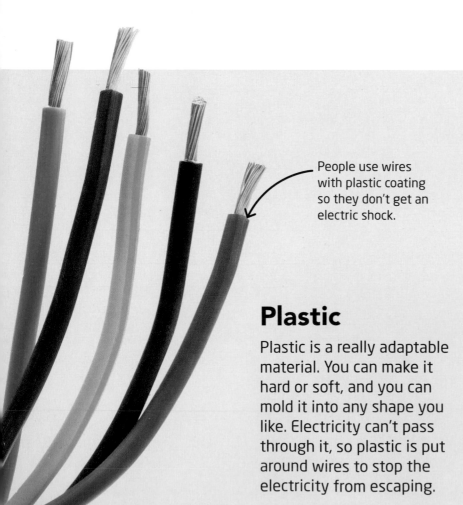

People use wires with plastic coating so they don't get an electric shock.

Plastic

Plastic is a really adaptable material. You can make it hard or soft, and you can mold it into any shape you like. Electricity can't pass through it, so plastic is put around wires to stop the electricity from escaping.

Wood

Wood is a strong material. It lasts a long time and doesn't break easily, so it is great for making furniture and musical instruments. Heat and electricity don't pass through wood very well.

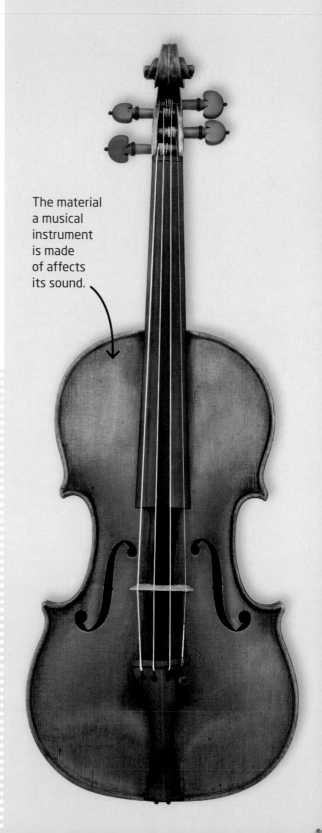

The material a musical instrument is made of affects its sound.

Fabric

Fabrics are woven from materials like wool and lycra. We wrap fabrics around our bodies to wear as clothing because they are flexible. Fabrics can help to keep us warm, or stretch to fit close to our skin.

Lycra is a stretchy fiber made in a factory.

Wool is a fiber that grows on sheep. It feels soft and keeps us warm on cold days.

Some metals are magnetic.

Metal

Metal is both strong and malleable, which means you can hammer it into shape without it breaking. It's great for molding into things you need to be tough, like the frame of a car.

Glass

We can see through glass even though it is solid. That means we can have windows in our homes without letting the cold in. Glass is also used in glasses to improve eyesight by bending light in just the right way.

Strongest material

Most people think diamond is the strongest material, but that depends on how you measure strength. Diamond is hard to crush, but not as hard to pull apart. This is called its tensile strength. Humanmade materials like graphene easily beat diamond in tensile strength.

Plastic bag puzzle

Scientists are curious people. When you question everything, you can find mysteries all around you that need a scientific explanation. Take a plastic shopping bag for example...

2
Scrunch up the square lengthwise, or holding the top and bottom, and try to pull it into two pieces.

Pull as hard as you can, but the bag probably won't rip.

Cut out a big square panel from a thin plastic shopping bag.

Do the pull test

1

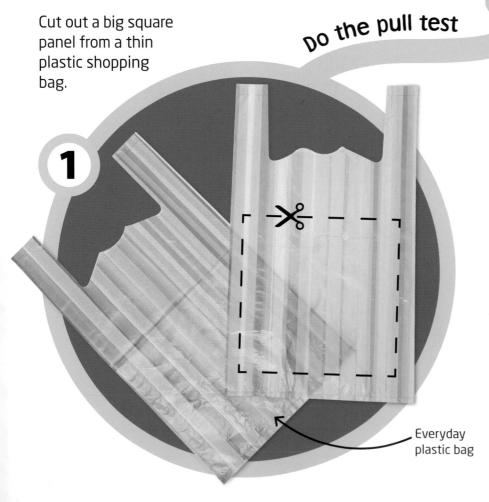

Everyday plastic bag

3
Unscrunch the square or cut out a new one. Scrunch it the other way, holding the two sides this time. Now try to pull it into two pieces.

Why does it break?

The plastic used in plastic shopping bags is made of lots of polymers. A polymer is a long chain of atoms tightly locked together. These chains are very strong, but the force that keeps one chain next to another is quite weak, so it's possible to separate them. In a plastic bag, all the chains are lined up in one direction.

It's much easier to separate the chains from one another widthwise.

Strong

Weak

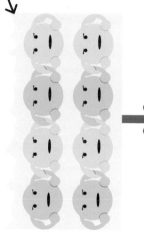

It's hard to break the strong chains lengthwise.

Try again

Scrunched the opposite way...

... it should break easily!

Ice cube trick

Here's a fun way to fool your friends. Put some ice cubes in a glass of water, then ask a friend to pick one up with a piece of string. It's impossible! Unless you know the trick...

1 Wet one end of a piece of string by dipping it into the glass of water and ice cubes.

The glass should be filled to the very top.

Lay the wet end of your string over an ice cube floating at the top of the glass. Now sprinkle a little bit of salt over it.

Wait for one minute

Add salt

2

Try more or less salt if the trick doesn't work first time.

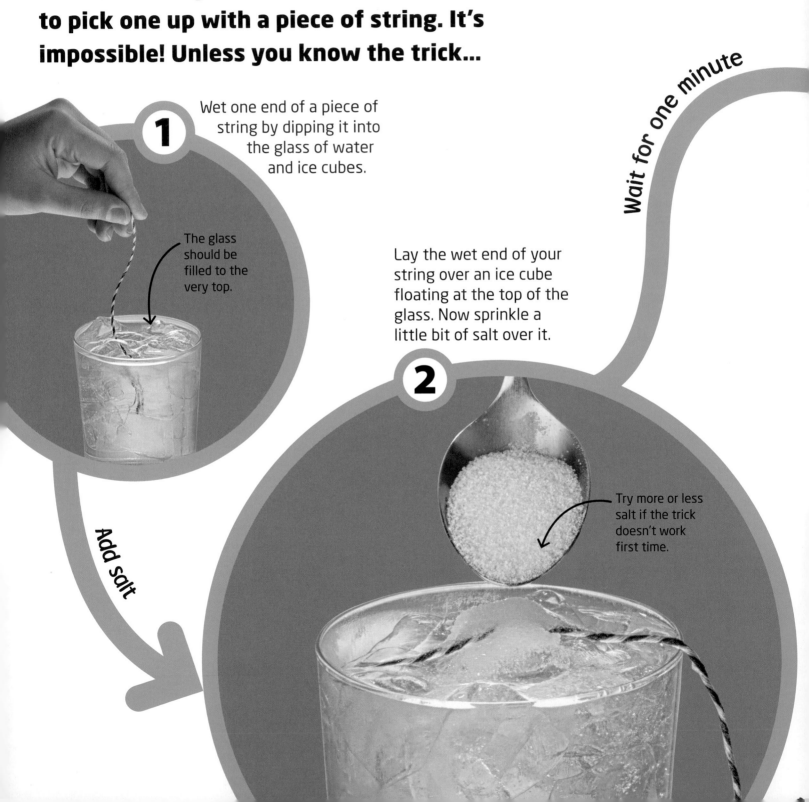

3

After a minute, lift up the string. You should find the ice cube is attached, and you can lift it out of the glass!

What's special about salt?

Frozen water normally melts at 32°F (0°C). Adding salt lowers the melting point, allowing your ice cube to melt. The melting ice makes the water around it colder—so once the salt has spread throughout the water a bit, the water re-freezes around the string.

A salt truck sprays salt on the roads in winter to melt the slippery ice.

Now try...

Can you make an ice cube necklace? Use a big bowl of water, and put in loads of ice cubes. How many can you get on a string at the same time?

Fill a clear plastic bottle about a third of the way with water, and add some food coloring.

1

Food coloring

Fizzy vitamin tablet

The cap must be kept off the bottle.

Vegetable oil

2

Fill with vegetable oil

Fill the bottle to the top with vegetable oil. It won't mix with the water. Drop in a vitamin tablet that will make the water become fizzy and bubble up.

Watch what happens

Make a bubble bottle

Really creative scientists love to put things together that don't normally mix. For example, oil and water don't combine. But when you try putting them together in this activity, something amazing will happen.

The contents of the bottle may bubble over the top.

What's making the bubbles?

The tablet is made of a mixture of chemicals. When you add water, the chemicals make bubbles of a gas called carbon dioxide. These bubbles float to the top because they are lighter than the liquids. As they rise through the oil, they pull some of the colored water with them.

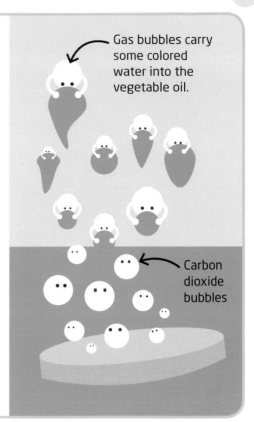

Gas bubbles carry some colored water into the vegetable oil.

Carbon dioxide bubbles

Gas bubble rising

Now try...

Add some raspberries or other small, light fruits that will float between the water and oil. What happens to them when you add the tablet?

3

Watch the colored water tumble up and down through the oil, making cool shapes that change before your eyes!

1 Put pineapple pieces into a small bowl, and pieces of other fruits into two other small bowls. Mix gelatin using the instructions on the package. Pour it over the fruit, and place the bowls in the fridge to set.

Wait a few hours

Pineapple
gelatin

Some of the best science happens when experiments go wrong. If you don't get the result you expected, maybe you've found something new! Even with a simple task, like making gelatin, things may not go to plan...

What's special about pineapple?

Gelatin sets because it is made of really long chemicals that tangle up and stick together. But pineapple contains a special chemical called bromelain. Bromelain's job is to break up long chemicals like the ones in set gelatin. This is why the pineapple gelatin doesn't set!

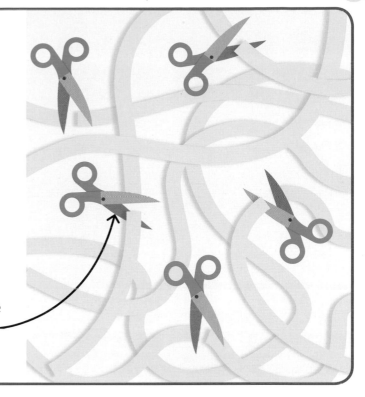

Bromelain acts like scissors, cutting up the long chemical strands.

Orange pieces set in gelatin

Strawberry pieces set in gelatin

The gelatin with the pineapple in it won't have set— it's still runny.

Now try...

Try eating chunks of pineapple. Some people find it can make their mouths feel a little sore. They may think it's because of citric acid in the fruit, but it's actually the bromelain!

2 After a few hours, take the bowls out of the fridge and see if the gelatin has set. Were all your creations successful?

Marie Curie

Chemist & physicist • Born in 1867 • From Poland

Marie Curie's parents were teachers who showed her the importance of learning and being curious. Curie's curiosity led her to find new elements that changed science forever. She also changed how we identify and treat illnesses.

Lab work

Curie's discovery of radioactivity is one of the most important scientific discoveries in history. An object that is radioactive gives off strong rays of energy and particles. Curie experimented with these invisible rays, which are called radiation.

Marie Curie working in her laboratory

Radioactive notebook

Curie spent her adult life surrounded by radiation. To this day her notes are stored in a lead-lined box because they are still radioactive and dangerous!

X-ray units

Curie figured out how to set up mobile X-ray units on the battlefields in World War I. These units helped surgeons to X-ray soldiers for bullets and fractures, and ultimately to save lives. She even drove one of the X-ray ambulances herself.

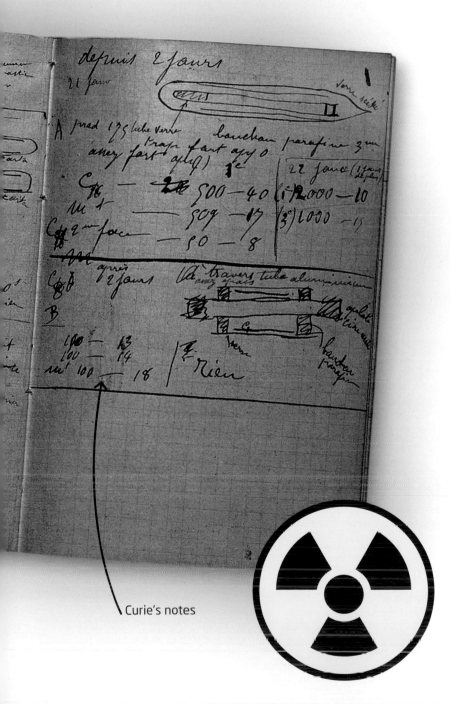

Curie's notes

Nobel Prizes

Marie Curie won the Nobel Prize twice! In 1903, she won the physics prize with Henri Becquerel and her husband, Pierre. She won the chemistry prize in 1911 for her discovery of two radioactive elements: polonium and radium.

Death

Because radioactivity was a new discovery, people didn't yet know the dangers. Curie died of a bone disease brought on by exposure to radiation.

Weather

Oceans

Snow

Poles

Earth

Earth is the place we call home, a planet covered in towering mountains, thick rainforests, and deep oceans. It provides us with the energy we need to live, so it's important for scientists to understand how the Earth works.

Mountains

Tornadoes

Water cycle

Sunlight

Rivers

Wind

Weather

People love talking about the weather. Is it hot or cold, sunny or cloudy, windy or calm? Is it raining or snowing? These are ways of describing the atmosphere around us. But where do wind and rain come from? What about other types of weather? Scientists take a closer look at the weather around them.

Rain

Rain clouds form when humid air, or air that contains lots of water particles, rises up and cools. Water particles clump together in the cooler air, forming droplets. These droplets fall to the ground as rain.

Lightning

Storm clouds are made up of tiny particles of frozen water whizzing around. When they bump into one another, they create electricity. This electricity gathers at the bottom of the cloud, and some of it jumps down to the ground as lightning.

There are 40 to 50 lightning strikes every second around the world.

Snow

If it's cold enough, the water inside clouds will form ice crystals instead of water droplets. When the ice crystals fall to the ground, so long as they don't melt on the way, they fall as snow. Sometimes the ice crystals stick together to form larger snowflakes.

Rainbow

Rainbows are rare because you need rain and sunshine at the same time to see one. Rainbows are caused by sunlight bouncing off droplets of rain. The rain splits the sunlight into different colors.

Wind

Wind is just the movement of air. Scientists predict which direction the wind will blow by looking at changes in temperature. Wind often blows from cold to hot places.

Cold at the poles

When the Sun's rays hit the Earth near the Equator, which is an imaginary line around the Earth's middle, they land on a small area. When they hit near the north and south poles, they are spread over a bigger area. This means the same amount of heat is shared over more space. That's why it gets colder as you get closer to the poles and much warmer nearer the Equator.

Sunlight is spread over a larger area near the poles.

Sunlight lands on a smaller area near the Equator.

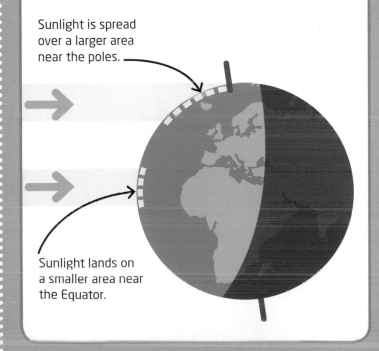

Make a tornado

Great scientists take what they've learned about one thing and use it to teach themselves about something else. For example, a scientist who learns about tornadoes can use this knowledge to examine liquid spinning down the drain of a sink, or even a jar of soapy water!

Spin the jar

2

Hold the jar with one hand on top and one on the bottom. Quickly move the jar around and around in a circular motion to get the liquid inside spinning.

1

Fill a jar with water and a little dishwashing liquid. Put the lid on tight. Give the jar a good shake, then let the water settle. You will see a thick layer of bubbles.

Try adding different amounts of dish-washing liquid. Do the results change?

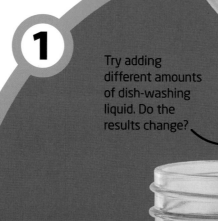

Watch the tornado go!

The tornado is wider at the top and narrower at the bottom.

What happens?

Moving the jar in a circle forces the water to the sides, but the walls of the jar keep it in, causing it to spin. Gravity pulls the water down at the same time, so you end up with a funnel shape. Real tornadoes, like the ones in these pictures, can spin as fast as 300 mph (480 kph)!

3

Set the jar down on a table. As the bubbles spin, the shape they make will change. What do you see?

Solar tower

Scientists love figuring out how things work, and their discoveries can benefit us all. Today scientists are working hard to solve some of the world's biggest problems, such as finding new ways to make energy. Here's one simple way you can harness the energy of the Sun.

Stick the tube together with tape.

First make four cuts from the corners that go two-thirds the way to the center.

Make the tube

Then fold one corner at a time into the middle and glue in place.

1 Cut out a square of paper about 4 in (10 cm) wide. Fold into a fan following these steps.

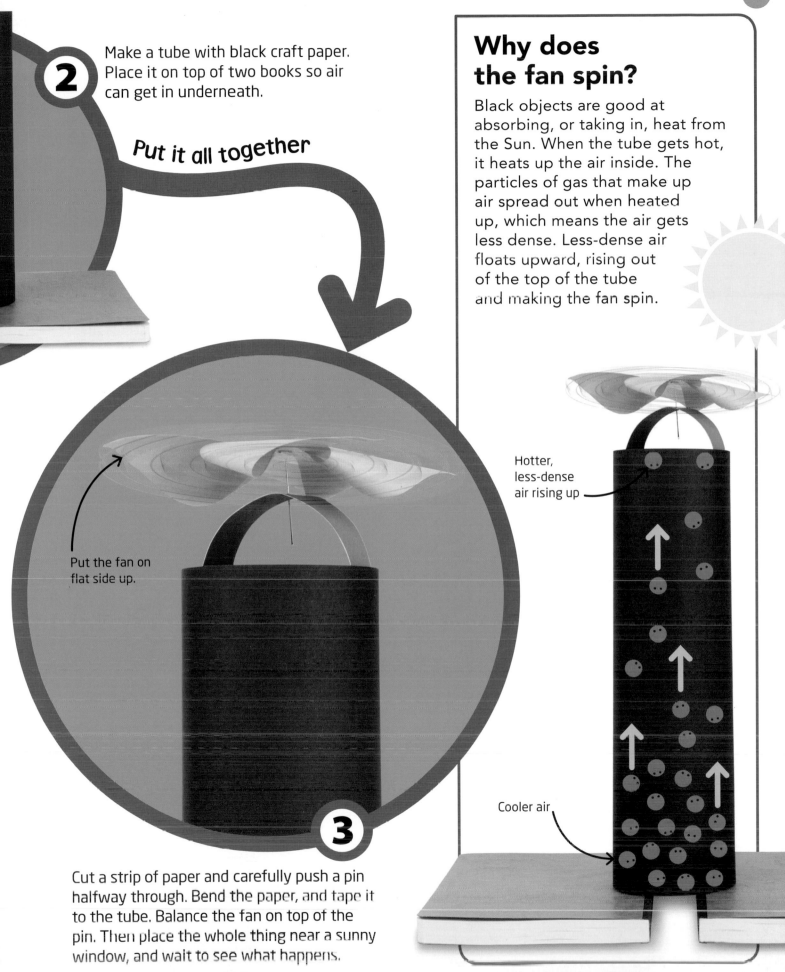

2 Make a tube with black craft paper. Place it on top of two books so air can get in underneath.

Put it all together

Put the fan on flat side up.

3

Cut a strip of paper and carefully push a pin halfway through. Bend the paper, and tape it to the tube. Balance the fan on top of the pin. Then place the whole thing near a sunny window, and wait to see what happens.

Why does the fan spin?

Black objects are good at absorbing, or taking in, heat from the Sun. When the tube gets hot, it heats up the air inside. The particles of gas that make up air spread out when heated up, which means the air gets less dense. Less-dense air floats upward, rising out of the top of the tube and making the fan spin.

Hotter, less-dense air rising up

Cooler air

The water cycle

When you drink a glass of water it's already been drunk many times before. In fact, it's even been drunk by a few dinosaurs! That's because there's only so much water on Earth, and it goes through a natural recycling process called the water cycle.

Clouds form

The warm vapor rises and cools. The cooled vapor moves slowly and sticks to dust particles in the air. As more vapor sticks to dust, water droplets or ice crystals grow, forming clouds.

Evaporation

When the Sun heats up the oceans, some water at the surface gets hot enough to escape into the air as tiny invisible particles called vapor. This is called evaporation.

Back to the ocean

Streams and rivers flow downhill, eventually returning water to the ocean. Some water evaporates before it gets there, but it's only a tiny amount.

Why is the sea salty?

Rivers pick up a tiny bit of salt from the rocks they flow over and carry it to the sea. But when water evaporates from the oceans, the salt is left behind. So salt is being added to the sea all the time, but it can never leave, making the sea saltier and saltier.

River flowing over rocks

Wind moves the clouds through the sky.

Rain

When these water droplets or ice crystals grow big enough, they fall out of the sky as rain or snow, depending on how cold it is.

Snow melts

Water that falls as snow may eventually melt and join the rainwater in streams, rivers, lakes, and water under the ground.

Attach to cork

1

Hold a needle by the part with a hole in it, called the eye. Rub the north end of a bar magnet (sometimes colored red) over the needle 50 times in one direction. Lift the magnet away from the needle after each stroke.

Make a compass

Legend has it that a Greek shepherd discovered magnetism 4,000 years ago when metal in his shoe stuck to a rock. Then someone noticed these rocks, now called magnets, always pointed in the same direction—the compass was born! Here's how you can make your own.

2 Attach the needle to a cork with some tape or sticky putty.

Float the cork

3 Fill a bowl with water, and float the cork in the center of the bowl. The needle will line up in a north–south direction, with the eye of the needle pointing north.

Eye of the needle pointing north

Point of the needle pointing south

How do magnets work?

Metals have lots of tiny particles moving around inside them called electrons. Some of these electrons are free to move around and they act like tiny magnets. Normally they're all pointing in different directions, so usually the metal has no magnetic pull in any one direction. But if all those tiny electron magnets are lined up in the same direction, they make a magnet.

Inside the needle
When you rub the end of a magnet against a needle, you cause all of the needle's electrons to line up in the same direction.

After rubbing the magnet on the needle, the electrons are lined up. The needle is now magnetic.

On a regular needle, the electrons aren't lined up. There is no magnetic pull.

Giant magnet The Earth itself is magnetic, like a huge bar magnet. That's why a compass needle points north—it lines up with the Earth's magnetic field lines.

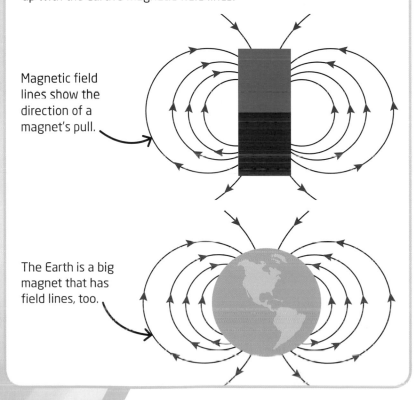

Magnetic field lines show the direction of a magnet's pull.

The Earth is a big magnet that has field lines, too.

Structure
of the Earth

The deepest hole ever dug goes down 7.5 miles (12 km). That may seem like a lot, but it's less than one thousandth of the width of the entire planet. So what's beneath that, and how did scientists figure it out?

Crust

The crust is the Earth's hard, cold outer layer. It's between 3 and 30 miles (5 and 50 km) thick and split into seven pieces called tectonic plates. These plates move against each other in jolts that sometimes cause earthquakes.

Mantle

This is the thickest layer at 1,800 miles (2,900 km). It's made of magma, which is semi-melted rock that flows really slowly. The temperature in the mantle varies from 900 to 1,600°F (500 to 900°C).

Outer core

The outer core is a layer of liquid iron and nickel, which are types of metal, about 1,400 miles (2,260 km) thick. It's about 9,000°F (5,000°C)—much hotter than the mantle, but not quite as hot as the inner core.

Volcanoes

Sometimes gaps in the Earth's crust allow magma just under the surface to be pushed out. This is called a volcanic eruption. The spot on the surface where it happens is called a volcano.

How do we know what's inside?

Earthquakes create shock waves that travel through the liquid and solid layers of the Earth at different speeds. Scientists figured out the Earth's structure by measuring how long it takes the waves to get to different places around the world.

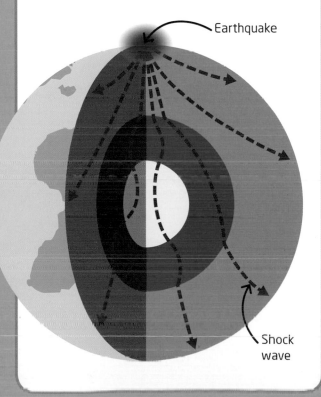

Earthquake

Shock wave

Inner core

The inner core is a solid ball of iron and nickel 760 miles (1,220 km) deep. It is a sizzling 9,700°F (5,400°C). Scientists think the inner core is slowly growing because the Earth is cooling, and this is starting to turn the outer core from liquid to solid.

Dip some string in

1

Put a few spoonfuls of Epsom salt into a glass. Pour in hot tap water and begin stirring. Keep adding salt and stirring until the salt doesn't mix into the water anymore.

Some of the salt may turn solid again as the water cools.

Grow crystals

People spend a lot of time and money looking for tiny crystals that form deep underground, such as diamonds. But with a little bit of knowledge, you can grow your own crystals at home.

2

Pour the salt water into a clean glass leaving any undissolved salt behind. Tie some string to a pencil. Place the pencil on top of the glass, letting the string hang down into the water.

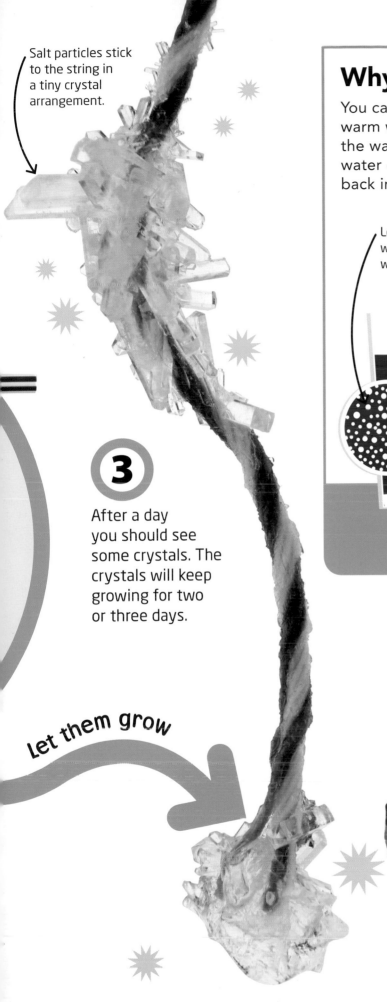

Salt particles stick to the string in a tiny crystal arrangement.

3

After a day you should see some crystals. The crystals will keep growing for two or three days.

Let them grow

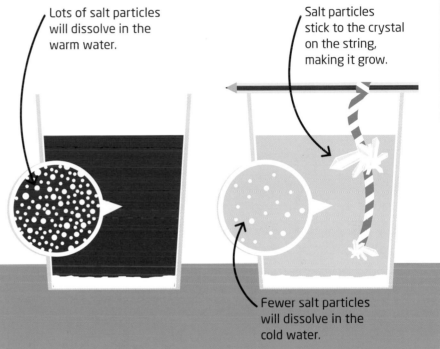

Why do the crystals form?

You can dissolve a lot more Epsom salt into warm water than cold water. In other words, the warm water can hold more salt. As the water cools down, some of the salt turns back into solid crystals on the string.

Lots of salt particles will dissolve in the warm water.

Salt particles stick to the crystal on the string, making it grow.

Fewer salt particles will dissolve in the cold water.

Jewels

Most natural crystals form in cooling magma just under the Earth's crust and take millions of years to grow. They start as a small crystal, and slowly more and more particles are added.

Natural crystals look quite rough until they're polished.

Raw crystals

Polished and cut crystals

Towel mountain

Scientists like to build models of the world that they can play with and explore. Processes that take millions of years in real life, like mountains forming, will take just a few seconds in a model like this one.

1 Lay a few towels down, one on top of the other. Put a large cardboard box on either side.

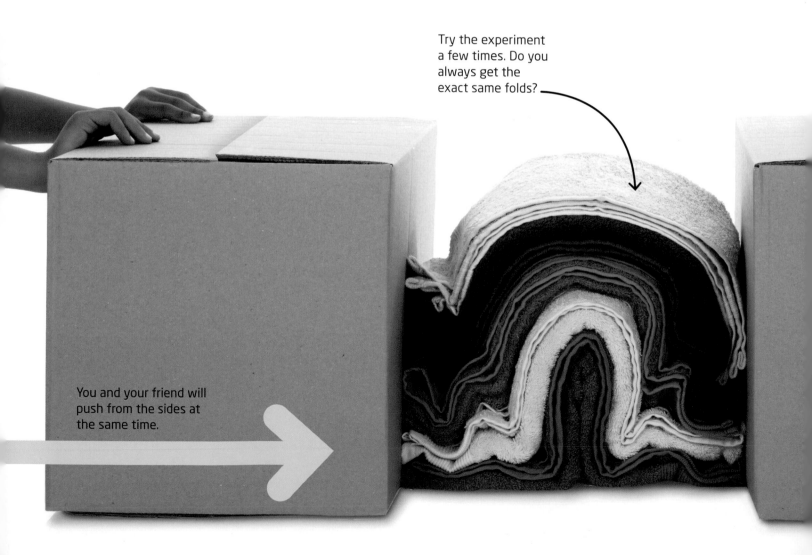

Try the experiment a few times. Do you always get the exact same folds?

You and your friend will push from the sides at the same time.

Use different colored towels so you can see the layers clearly.

Push the boxes

2 Ask a friend to help you push the two boxes in toward the middle. The towels will bunch up and fold in interesting ways, just like mountains in real life.

What are fold mountains?

The outer layer of the Earth is made up of separate sections called tectonic plates. These plates sometimes push against each other. When they do, layers of rock can crumple and fold up. This forms a type of mountain called a fold mountain.

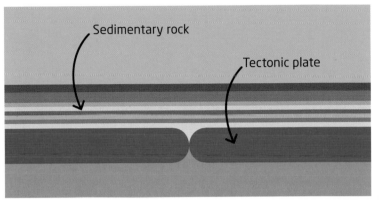

Sedimentary rock

Tectonic plate

Tectonic plates Bits of earth called sediment have settled above the boundary, or meeting spot, of the tectonic plates. Over time this forms layers of sedimentary rock.

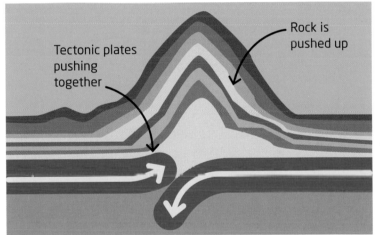

Rock is pushed up

Tectonic plates pushing together

Fold mountains When the tectonic plates are pushed together, the sedimentary rock crumples upward, forming fold mountains.

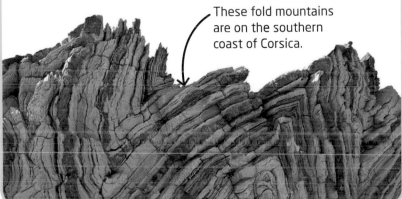

These fold mountains are on the southern coast of Corsica.

Energy

chain reactions

Circuits

Heat

Physics

Scientists who study physics want to understand how the Universe works— why things move, how they interact with one another, and why one thing leads to another. This means looking at energy, forces, and particles.

Forces

Electricity

Light

Waves

Sound

Gravity

What is energy?

There are different types of energy, but they all have one thing in common: the ability to make something happen. Scientists call this the ability to "do work." Luckily for us, that "work" can be something fun—like sending a roller coaster down a big drop!

Electricity

Electrical energy powers much of our technology. The electrical energy inside a battery, for example, can do things like make a toy car move. Electricity that flows through big power wires brings energy to our homes.

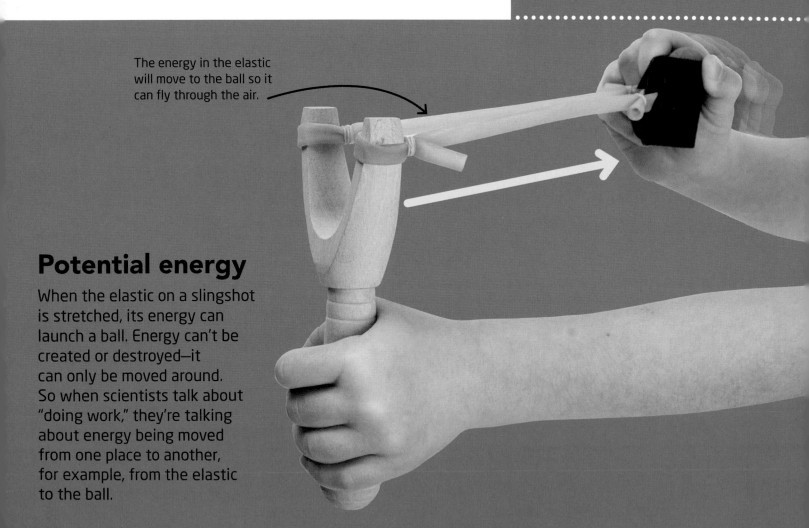

The energy in the elastic will move to the ball so it can fly through the air.

Potential energy

When the elastic on a slingshot is stretched, its energy can launch a ball. Energy can't be created or destroyed—it can only be moved around. So when scientists talk about "doing work," they're talking about energy being moved from one place to another, for example, from the elastic to the ball.

Gravity and movement

When a roller coaster car is at the top of the track, we say it has something called gravitational potential energy. That means it has the potential to be pulled down by gravity. When it rides back down the track, that energy is changed to the energy of movement, which is called kinetic energy.

Heat

Something is hot when the particles inside it are moving back and forth really quickly. When you rub things together, they get hot—this is a way of converting kinetic energy into heat. Heat can also be created by a chemical reaction, such as when wood is burned to make fire.

Changing energy

Most of the energy we use on Earth first comes from the Sun. In a way, that means all of us are solar-powered! Once on Earth, energy is never lessened or destroyed, but it does change form quite a few times along its path. Here's one example of the journey energy can take.

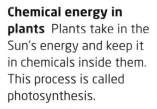

Heat Energy comes to Earth from the Sun in the form of heat and light. Some of it gets reflected back into space, but most is taken in by the Earth.

Chemical energy in plants Plants take in the Sun's energy and keep it in chemicals inside them. This process is called photosynthesis.

Chemical energy in people When we eat fruit and vegetables, we take the chemical energy of the plant into our bodies.

Kinetic energy We use our muscles to change the chemical energy in our bodies into movement. This movement is kinetic energy.

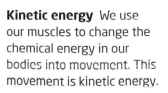

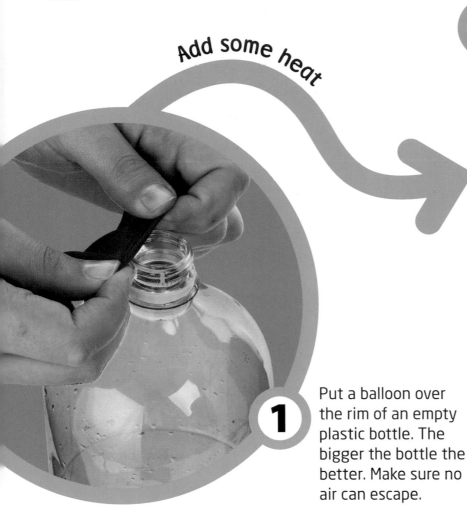

Add some heat

1 Put a balloon over the rim of an empty plastic bottle. The bigger the bottle the better. Make sure no air can escape.

2 Fill up a tub with warm water. It shouldn't be boiling hot—warm water from the tap is good enough to make this experiment work. Now, keeping your hand on the bottle, place it in the water. Watch and see what happens...

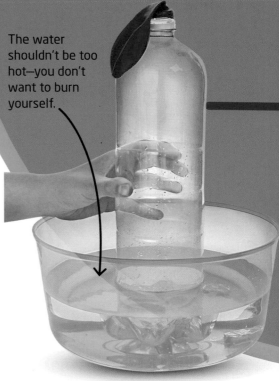

The water shouldn't be too hot—you don't want to burn yourself.

Hot-air balloon

Have you ever looked at a hot-air balloon flying through the sky and wondered how it stays up? The key is to add heat. But what exactly is going on? This simple activity will help you figure it out.

Why does the balloon expand?

At the start of the project, the air inside the bottle is the same temperature as the air outside it. Once the bottle is placed in warm water, however, it heats up the air inside the bottle.

Cold particles Air is made up of lots of tiny particles. When they are cold, they don't move around much.

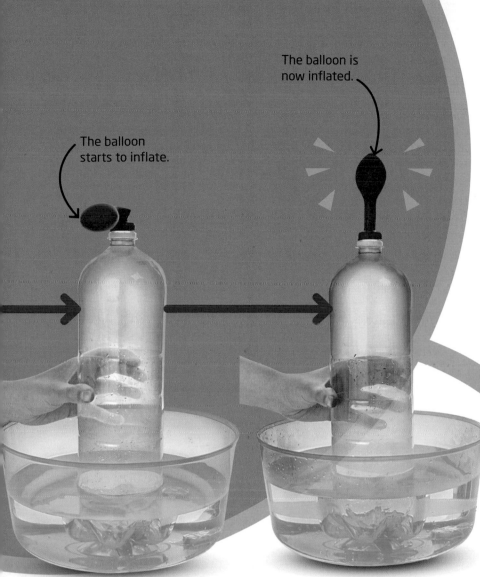

The balloon starts to inflate.

The balloon is now inflated.

In the real world

We've seen that warm air expands. In other words, it takes up more space without getting heavier—it becomes less dense. Less dense things float on top of more dense things, and this is the principle behind hot-air balloons—heat up the air in the balloon and watch it rise!

Time to chill

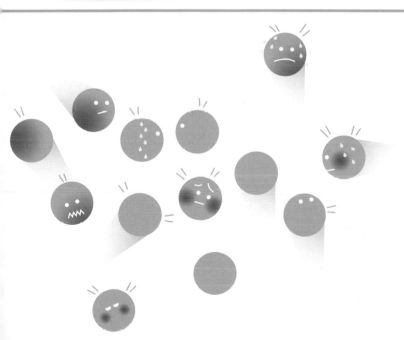

Warm particles When the air is heated up, the particles get more active, banging against each other and spreading out. This makes the air expand, pushing the balloon out!

3

Now take the bottle out of the warm water and put it in a new tub filled with ice cubes. The balloon deflates! Can you figure out why?

Flip the picture

When you turn on a light, it shines on everything in the room. Some of the light bounces off things and ends up in your eyes. That's how we see. But light doesn't always go in a straight line. This project shows how you can bend light and flip things around.

Find a glass

1 Draw two fish, one on top of the other, on a sheet of paper about the same width as a clear glass.

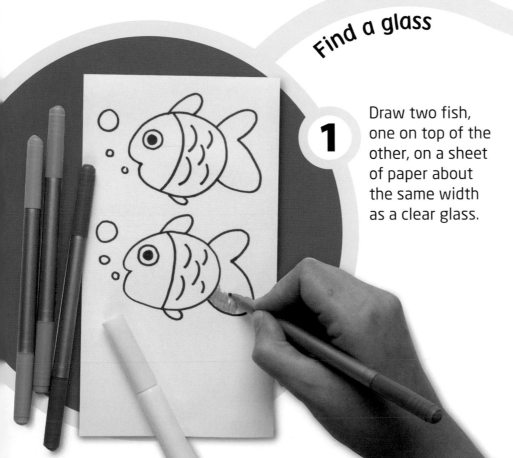

How does it flip?

When the light from the fish passes through the glass of water, it bends on the way in and on the way out. Because of the shape of the glass, it bends in just the right way to completely flip the image. Eye glasses work in the same way—they bend light in just the right way to give the wearer a clear image.

2

Put your drawing behind a clear glass. Slowly fill the glass with water and watch how the picture changes before your eyes!

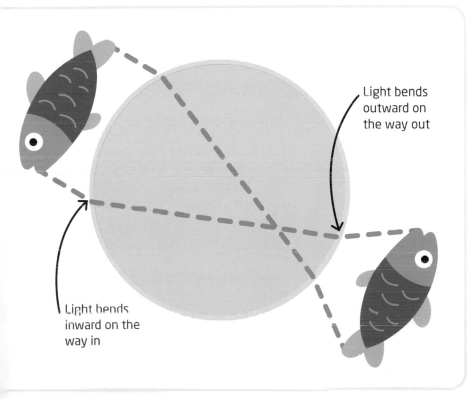

Light bends outward on the way out

Light bends inward on the way in

Now try...

Put your eye right up against the glass. The image should now be the right way around. Back away to find the spot where the image flips over.

Add the next stick

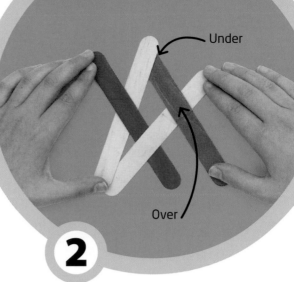

Under

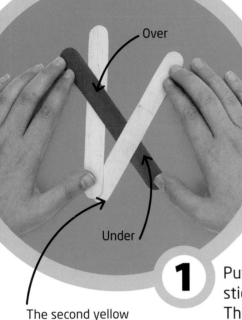

Over

Under

The second yellow stick is held under the first yellow stick.

1 Put three jumbo craft sticks together as shown. This is the start of a weave pattern.

Under

Over

2 The next stick, which is red in this picture, goes under and over as shown. Make sure one hand is holding the rest of the sticks in place.

3 The next stick, which is yellow in this picture, goes under and over as shown.

Building the weave on a carpet makes it easier to push new sticks under.

Stick
explosion

When you bend a jumbo craft stick, you are storing energy in it. When you let it go, the energy is released as movement, making the stick spring back. In this activity, you will weave together lots of craft sticks to create a movement explosion.

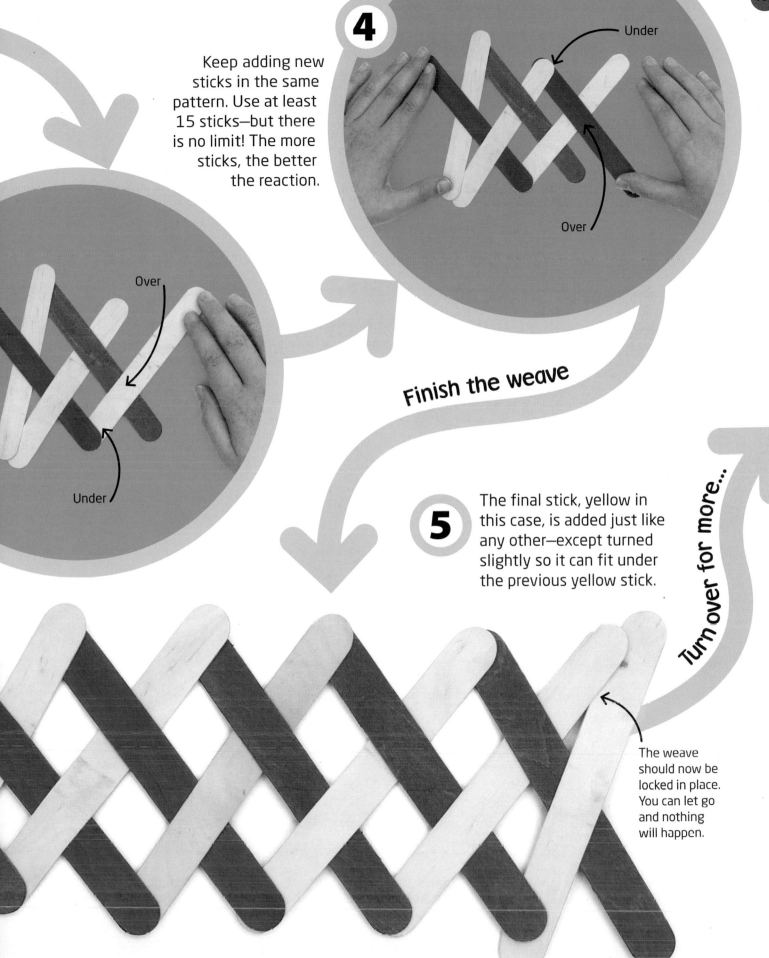

4 Keep adding new sticks in the same pattern. Use at least 15 sticks—but there is no limit! The more sticks, the better the reaction.

Under

Over

Over

Under

Finish the weave

5 The final stick, yellow in this case, is added just like any other—except turned slightly so it can fit under the previous yellow stick.

Turn over for more...

The weave should now be locked in place. You can let go and nothing will happen.

6 Each stick is holding the next stick in place. When you remove the first one, they will all fly out one after the other.

Some of the sticks push down as they are released...

... lifting the weave into the air!

The rising sticks travel down the weave as a wave.

What is a chain reaction?

The stick explosion is a great example of a chain reaction, where one action leads to the next. Another chain reaction is dominoes being knocked down in a line. Can you think of other examples?

One domino hits the next, continuing the chain reaction.

The explosion ends with a flourish!

7 When the wave of energy hits the end of the weave, the sticks will fly off in different directions. Be careful you don't get too close!

Singing
bike tire

When you clap your hands, the air in between is squeezed out at high speed. This movement of air travels outward in all directions. When it reaches your ears, it rattles your eardrums. Your brain picks this up as a short, sharp noise. Here, you will use this idea to make music.

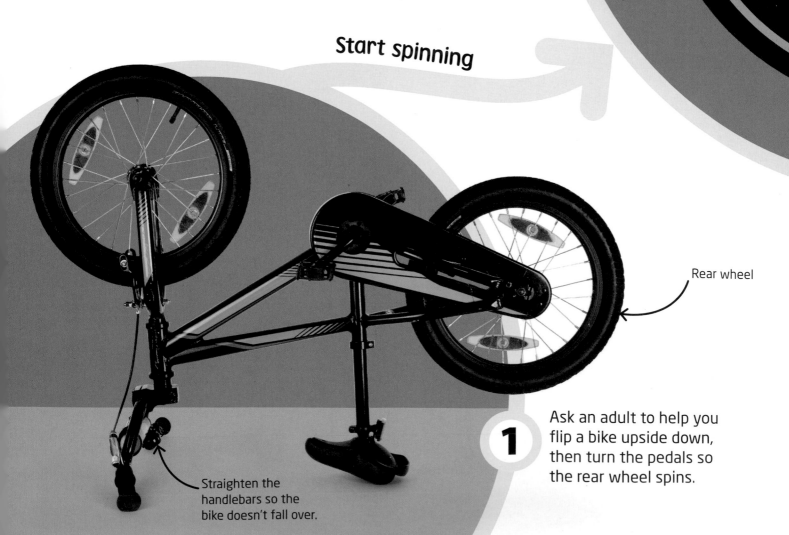

Start spinning

Rear wheel

Straighten the handlebars so the bike doesn't fall over.

1 Ask an adult to help you flip a bike upside down, then turn the pedals so the rear wheel spins.

2 While the wheel is spinning, push the end of a ruler against the tire. It should sound like a note being played on a musical instrument. Try spinning the wheel at different speeds—does it affect the sound?

What makes the sound?

When the ruler hits a bump, or tread, it's the same effect as clapping your hands—the air gets squeezed out. This happens again and again, so the air moves backward and forward, or vibrates, really quickly. When it reaches our ears, we hear it as a note.

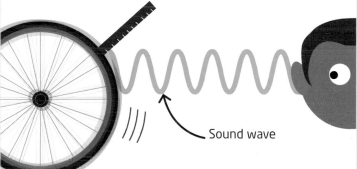

Sound wave

High pitch Spin the wheel quickly and the vibrations speed up. We hear this as a high note.

Low pitch Spin the wheel slowly and the vibrations slow down. We hear this as a low note.

Making music

To make different notes, you need to vibrate the air at different speeds. This is how musical instruments work. For example, a plucked guitar string wiggles back and forth, and vibrates the air around it.

Electricity

Electricity is used to power all sorts of things, from light bulbs to electric cars. You can think of it a bit like water flowing through a pipe. In place of water is electricity. It is made of lots of tiny particles called electrons, and instead of pipes, it flows through metal wires.

Wires

Wires are made of metal because metal is a good conductor, which means electricity flows through it easily. The metal usually used is copper.

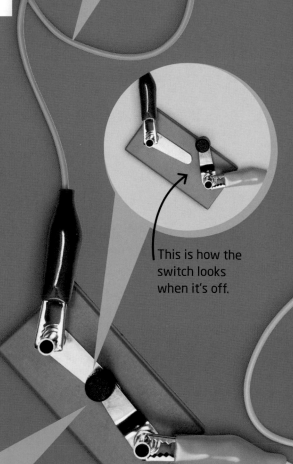

This is how the switch looks when it's off.

Simple circuit

Let's look at a simple circuit to see how electricity works. A circuit is just a loop that electricity can flow around. Along the way, the electricity will pass through a few "components," such as a battery and a light bulb.

Switch

A switch is something that breaks the loop of an electric circuit. Breaking the loop stops electricity flowing around the circuit. This is how light switches work.

Off When the loop is broken, electrons cannot flow around the circuit. If the circuit is broken, the light bulb will be off.

On When the loop is complete, electrons can flow around the circuit. If the circuit is complete, the light bulb will be on.

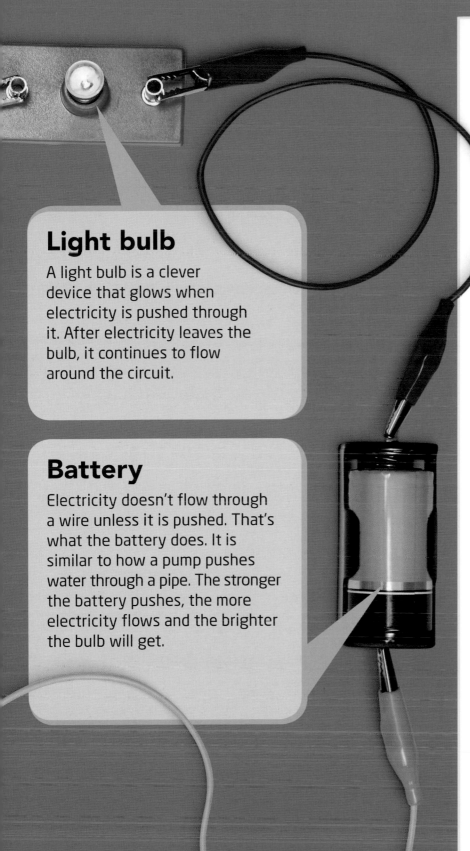

Light bulb

A light bulb is a clever device that glows when electricity is pushed through it. After electricity leaves the bulb, it continues to flow around the circuit.

Battery

Electricity doesn't flow through a wire unless it is pushed. That's what the battery does. It is similar to how a pump pushes water through a pipe. The stronger the battery pushes, the more electricity flows and the brighter the bulb will get.

Creating electricity

If you've ever used a wind-up flashlight, you'll know that you can make electricity by turning something around. Most electricity in our homes is made in the same way. For example, some power plants burn coal. This creates steam, which turns a wheel or rotor, making electricity.

Fossil fuels Fossil fuels, such as coal, oil, and gas, are made of the fossilised remains of ancient plants and animals.

Nuclear power Electricity is generated in nuclear power plants by releasing the energy inside atoms.

Renewable energy Wind farms use wind to turn giant blades, creating electricity. Solar panels turn sunlight directly into electricity.

Isaac Newton

Physicist • Born in 1643 • From the UK

Isaac Newton came up with laws that describe how things move. He put them all in a famous book called *Philosophiæ Naturalis Principia Mathematica*. In the book Newton described how the universe worked using math. It's one of the most important science books ever written.

Gravity from the Sun makes the planets move around it.

Gravity

Before Newton we didn't know why objects fall to the ground, or why the planets travel around the Sun. When Newton thought about these two things together, he realized they were both caused by gravity. Gravity is a force that pulls objects together, and Newton came up with math to describe it.

Falling apple Newton said he came up with his theory of gravity when he saw an apple fall from a tree.

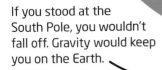

If you stood at the South Pole, you wouldn't fall off. Gravity would keep you on the Earth.

Gravity from the Earth keeps the Moon from floating off into space.

Arch rivals

Newton and scientist Robert Hooke wrote each other letters about gravity. Later they argued over who first discovered it, and became enemies. In fact, after Hooke died, Newton may have burned the only painting of him!

Every object in the universe has its own gravity.

Colors of the rainbow

Newton also discovered that white light is made up of all the colors in a rainbow mixed together. Using a tool called a prism to bend light, he found that different colors bend different amounts, making a rainbow.

Prism

The light is split into a rainbow of colors.

Light goes in

Paper planes

When engineers design airplanes, they test each idea over and over to see how they can make it better. Even if you're making paper planes, like the one in this activity, you'll find a little trial and error can go a long way.

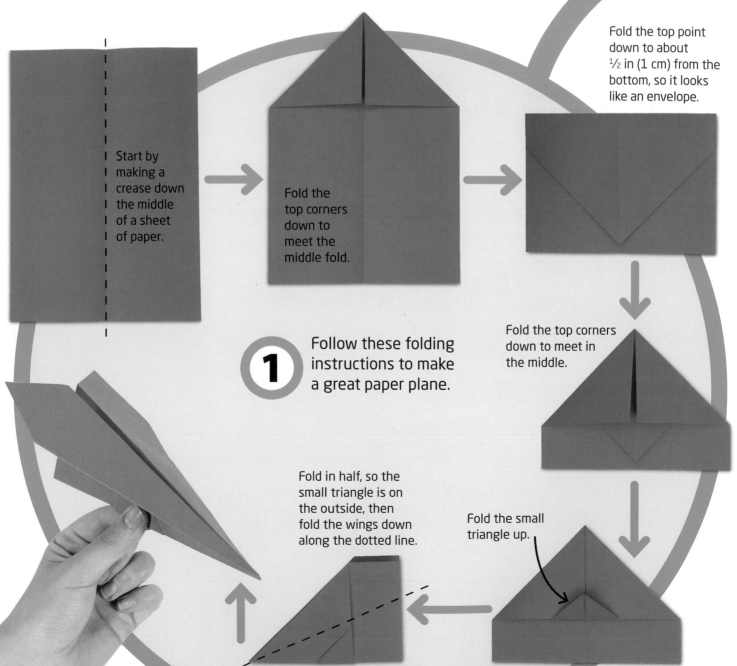

Throw it!

Fold the top point down to about ½ in (1 cm) from the bottom, so it looks like an envelope.

Start by making a crease down the middle of a sheet of paper.

Fold the top corners down to meet the middle fold.

1 Follow these folding instructions to make a great paper plane.

Fold the top corners down to meet in the middle.

Fold in half, so the small triangle is on the outside, then fold the wings down along the dotted line.

Fold the small triangle up.

2 See how far you can throw the plane. Try throwing at different angles and speeds, and write down your results. What works best?

Watch your plane zoom through the air!

Does your plane fly straight or does it twirl?

Why does it fly?

The force of gravity pulls your plane down. You need another force, called lift, to push it back up. Lift is created when air is forced to move around the wings of a plane. Your paper plane slows down because of air resistance, called drag. When it slows down, it loses lift and falls. Real planes avoid this with an engine that's always pushing it on, creating a forward force called thrust. You create thrust for your paper plane when you throw it.

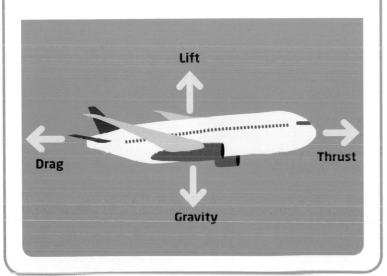

Lift

Drag

Thrust

Gravity

Now try...

Bend flaps into the back of your plane. Try pointing them up, then down, then a mixture of both. How is the flight of your plane affected? Don't forget to record your results!

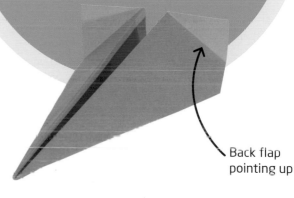

Back flap pointing up

Feel the force

If you rub two sheets of paper together, you'll find they slide over each other easily. That's because the force that stops things sliding over each other is quite small in this case. This force is called friction, and as you'll see in this activity, small bits of friction can really add up.

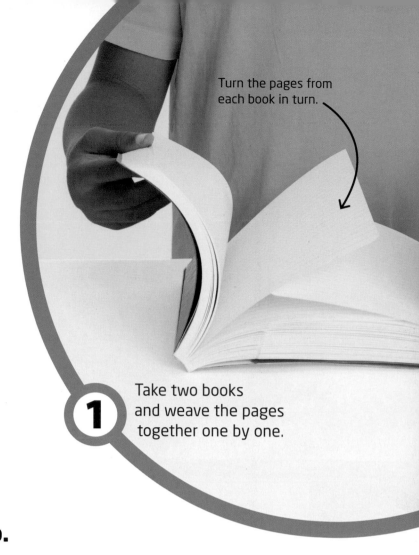

Turn the pages from each book in turn.

1 Take two books and weave the pages together one by one.

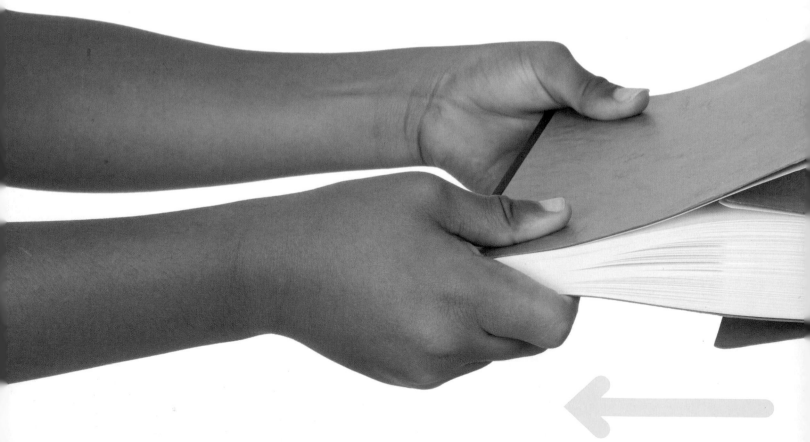

How does friction work?

Friction is the force that tries to stop one object from moving over another. Paper may look smooth, but up close there are lots of little bumps that can catch on another surface. This is one of the things that can contribute to friction. When you weave together the pages of two books, each page laying against another adds a little more friction until it becomes impossible to pull the books apart.

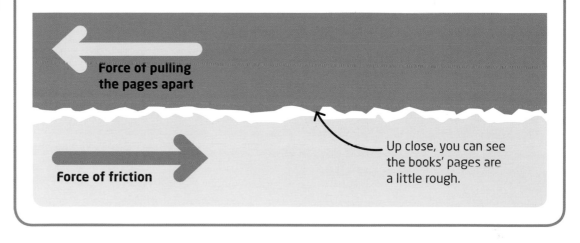

Force of pulling the pages apart

Force of friction

Up close, you can see the books' pages are a little rough.

Pull!

2 Try as hard as you can to pull the books apart. You can try it yourself, or ask a friend to help you for added strength.

Carefully drop some marbles into a bowl of water. They will sink straight to the bottom. Now roll some craft dough into a ball and drop it in. What happens?

1

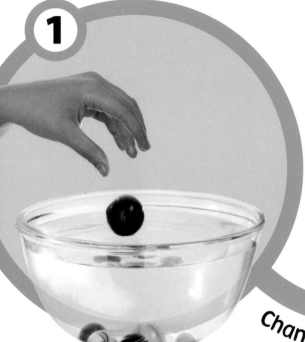

2 With a bit of crafty reshaping, you can make the dough float. Mold it into a boat shape with raised sides. Does it work?

Change the shape

Add some weight

Float the boat

If you drop a pebble in water, it will sink, but a giant passenger ship can easily float across the surface of the ocean. Why does one sink and one float? A good way to figure this out is with some marbles and craft dough.

3 Not only should your boat float, it should be able to take some passengers on board! Try adding a few marbles. How many can you load before the boat sinks?

Why doesn't it sink?

Archimedes was an Ancient Greek scientist who figured out why things float. He realized that when something sinks into water, it pushes some of that water out of the way, or displaces it. He worked out that an object will only sink if it's heavier than the water it displaces, otherwise it will float.

- Archimedes
- Born in 217 BCE
- From Greece

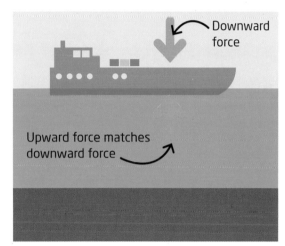

Floating Because of their shape, large ships are full of air, meaning they weigh the same or less than the water they displace. This creates an upward force called buoyancy.

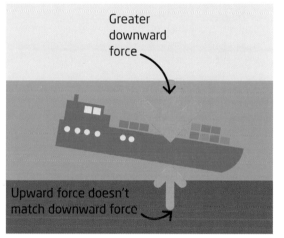

Sinking If a ship is carrying too much, or if disaster strikes and it takes water onboard, it will weigh more than the water it has displaced and will sink.

Now try...

Now that you've worked out that things float because of their shape, it's time to try out a few different boat designs. Which boat can take the most marbles onboard?

Secret shower

With a little bit of scientific knowledge, you can easily trick a friend. They will get a good soaking in this experiment, and it's all thanks to a strange thing that water can do.

Unscrew...

2

Fill the bottle with water and quickly screw on the cap. Do this over a sink, as water will come out of the holes until the cap is screwed on tightly.

Fill with water

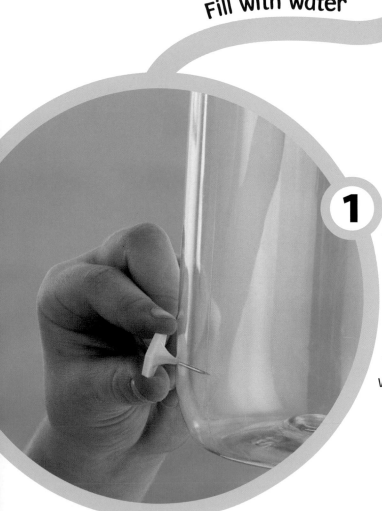

1

Take an empty plastic drink bottle, and carefully poke five or six holes about 1 in (3 cm) from the bottom with a pin.

How does it work?

For water to get out of the bottle, air needs to get in to replace it. But the tiny particles that make up water like to stick to one another and to the container's walls. This is called surface tension. It creates a barrier that stops air getting in. When the lid is on, no air can get in the top either. This means no water can escape. Taking off the lid lets more air in, allowing the water to fall out.

Surprise! Jets of water come squirting out.

Give the bottle to a friend and tell them to unscrew the cap. When they do, they'll be sprayed with water from the holes!

3

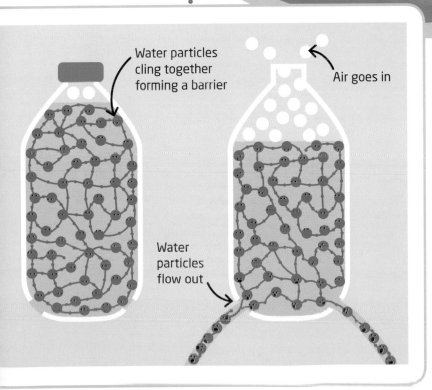

Water particles cling together forming a barrier

Air goes in

Water particles flow out

Now try...

How big can you make the holes before it stops working? Add some soap to reduce the surface tension. Does it make a difference to how big the holes can be?

Albert Einstein

Physicist • Born in 1879 • From Germany

Albert Einstein is one of the most famous scientists of all time. He managed to come up with answers to questions people hadn't even thought about asking! He developed one of the most important scientific equations ever, as well as a new theory of gravity that changed how we think about space and time.

Changing mass to energy

Einstein came up with the equation $E = mc^2$. This tells us that just a little bit of mass, which is related to how heavy something is, can be turned into a whole lot of energy.

Einstein said it is important to question everything.

Theory of gravity

Einstein's theory of gravity says that time moves more slowly for things that are in orbit around, or circling, the Earth. Our satellites have to take this into account or they wouldn't work!

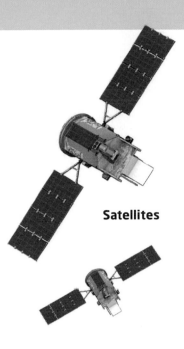

Satellites

Studying his brain

Seven hours after Einstein died, his brain was removed, weighed, and preserved. It has since been studied by scientists looking to explain why he was so smart, but nothing certain has been found.

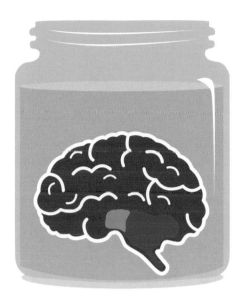

$$mc^2$$

What does it mean? This equation means that energy (E) is equal to the mass (m) of something multiplied by the speed of light (c) multiplied by the speed of light again (which is a really, really big number!).

Equation in action

When a nuclear bomb explodes, tiny atoms are split into even tinier pieces. As they split, energy is released. Even though the atoms have very little mass, we know from $E = mc^2$ that the explosion of energy will be huge.

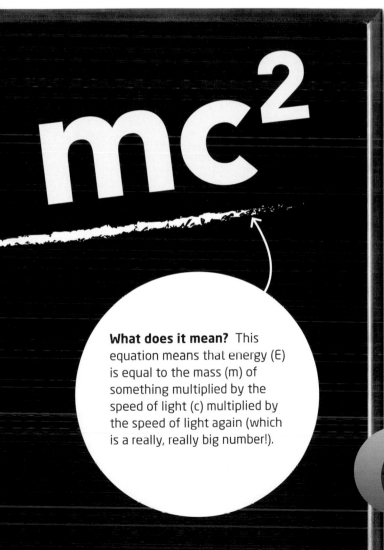

Exploration

Meteors

Phases

Craters

Space

Looking at the night sky has always inspired wonder. The lights we see in the sky are now known to be stars, planets, and galaxies. Science answers big questions about space, but it also uncovers new mysteries along the way.

The Solar System

The Solar System is made up of the Sun and everything that orbits, or travels around, it. The Solar System is huge. For example, the distance from the Earth to the Sun is 6,000 times the width of the Earth. In fact, the Solar System is so spread out that it's been bunched up quite a bit to make it fit on the page!

Mercury

Mercury is the smallest planet and the closest to the Sun. It has the shortest year (the amount of time it takes to go around the Sun), lasting only 88 Earth days.

The Sun

The Sun is our nearest star. It is so big that you could fit 1.3 million Earths inside it! It is mostly made up of the gases hydrogen and helium.

Venus

Even though Mercury is closer to the Sun, Venus is hotter. That's because Venus has a thick atmosphere that acts like a greenhouse, trapping heat in.

Earth

The third planet from the Sun is where we call home. It's just the right temperature for life to exist. On Earth, water doesn't boil away, or totally freeze over.

Jupiter

Jupiter is called a gas giant because it's mostly made of gas, with a tiny rocky bit in the middle. It is the biggest planet in the Solar System and it has more than 60 moons!

Uranus

All the planets in the Solar System spin, but for some reason Uranus spins on its side! Some scientists think it may have been knocked on its side by an Earth-sized object.

Neptune

A year on Neptune lasts 165 Earth years. This means no human has ever lived long enough to see it go all the way around the Sun!

Pluto used to be called a planet. Now it's called a dwarf planet.

Dwarf planets

In 2005, scientists discovered Eris, a new object in the Solar System that was bigger than Pluto. Instead of announcing the discovery of a new planet, they decided to create a new category to put it in—the dwarf planets. They then decided Pluto was a dwarf planet, too.

Mars

Mars looks reddish-brown because it's covered in rust! We have landed robots on Mars that send pictures and data back to us. It's even possible that we could live on Mars as it's not too hot or cold.

Saturn

This gas giant is famous for its enormous rings. They are made up of billions of chunks of ice and rock. Jupiter, Neptune, and Uranus have rings too, but they're very faint.

It's daytime where the Sun is shining.

shine a flashlight

1 Make a ball of modelling clay to represent Earth. It should be about the size of a tennis ball. Poke the tip of a pencil into it.

2 Turn out the lights, and shine a flashlight on the ball. This represents how the Sun shines on the Earth.

Nighttime

Create your own sunrise

People used to think the Sun circled around the Earth, making day and night. Thanks to scientists such as Galileo and Isaac Newton, we know this isn't true. Try building this model to see what's really going on.

You may need a friend to hold the flashlight for you.

What makes day and night?

As the Earth spins, parts of the planet move in and out of the Sun's light. The light parts are in daytime, and the dark parts are in nighttime. From our point of view on Earth, the Sun looks like it's moving around us. But it's actually the Earth spinning that makes night and day.

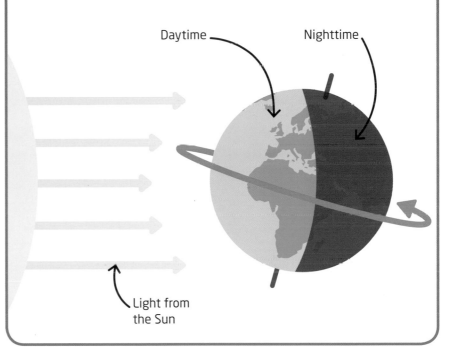

Daytime

Nighttime

Light from the Sun

Turn the pencil

Sunrise

Daytime

Now try making the Moon...

3

Put a dot on the ball to show where you live. Turn the pencil so Earth rotates counterclockwise, and watch the dot move into the flashlight's light, representing a sunrise.

Phases of the Moon

Like the Sun, the Moon appears and disappears at regular times. People didn't understand why until they put their scientific minds to it. We now know the Moon travels around the Earth. But why does the Moon appear to change shape?

Make a modelling-clay ball about a quarter of the width of the Earth ball. Then stick the tip of a pencil into it. This will represent the Moon.

1

Shine a flashlight

2

Turn off the lights. Hold the Moon out at arm's length, and ask a friend to shine a flashlight to represent the Sun. Move your body around the Moon to change your view of it. Watch as the shape appears to change.

Flashlight straight on
You'll see a full moon. Make sure your head isn't in the way of the light.

What are the phases?

As the Moon moves around the Earth, we see it being lit by the Sun from different angles. This makes the Moon appear to change shape. It's still round, it's just that we can't see the parts of it that are in darkness. These shapes are called the phases of the Moon, and they have different names.

New moon

Waxing crescent

First quarter

Waxing gibbous

Full moon

Waning gibbous

Last quarter

Waning crescent

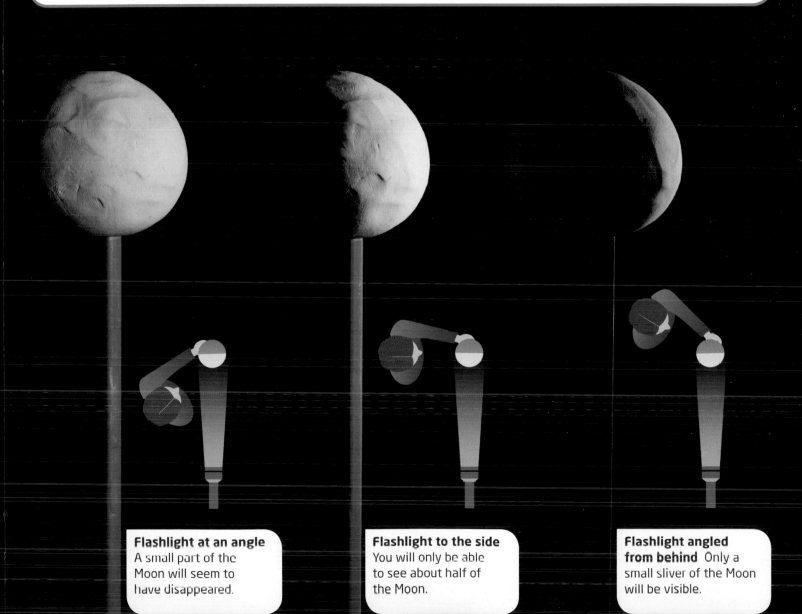

Flashlight at an angle A small part of the Moon will seem to have disappeared.

Flashlight to the side You will only be able to see about half of the Moon.

Flashlight angled from behind Only a small sliver of the Moon will be visible.

Mark the hours

At 8 o'clock, mark the shadow again and write an 8. Keep doing this once an hour until sunset, marking the shadow and writing the hour next to it.

2

At 8am

1

Poke a pencil through the middle of a paper plate. Place it upside down outside. At 7 o'clock in the morning, make a dot where the shadow of the pencil falls and write the number 7. If sunrise is after 7 o'clock, start the project later.

Once finished, you can use the shadow of the pencil to tell the time! Just be careful not to move the plate.

At 6pm

At 5pm

At 4pm

At 3pm

12
11
10
9
8
7

Make a sundial

Scientists build equipment to help them examine the world around them. The oldest clock ever built is probably the sundial and they're a lot of fun to make.

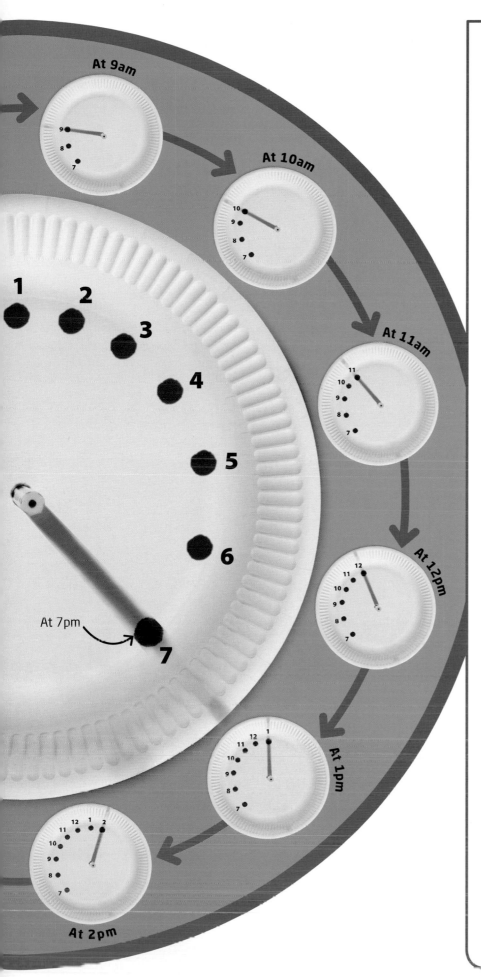

At 9am

At 10am

At 11am

At 12pm

At 1pm

At 2pm

At 7pm

1
2
3
4
5
6
7

Why does the shadow move?

Shadows cast by the Sun are always on the opposite side from the Sun. This means that as the Sun moves across the sky, the pencil shadow moves around the opposite side of the plate. It's the same movement every day, so once you've marked the times, you can use the sundial as a clock. The only time it won't work is when it's cloudy!

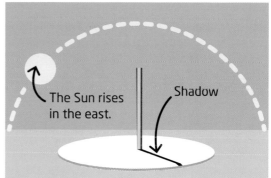

The Sun rises in the east.

Shadow

Sun rising

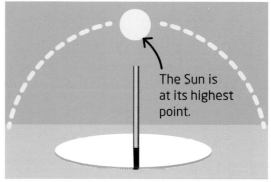

The Sun is at its highest point.

Midday

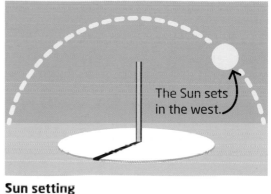

The Sun sets in the west.

Sun setting

Galileo

Astronomer • Born in 1564 • From Italy

Galileo completely changed our view of the Solar System. Albert Einstein called him the "father of modern science" because he combined thinking logically with doing experiments and making observations. His findings weren't always accepted by other people, and being outspoken got him into trouble.

The telescope

Galileo was the first astronomer to use a telescope to record observations about the Solar System. He made many amazing discoveries with a telescope, such as that the Milky Way galaxy is made of stars, the Moon has hills, Jupiter has moons, and the Sun has dark spots on its surface.

Sun

Geocentric People used to think that the Solar System was geocentric, which means Earth is at the center. Galileo proved this idea was wrong.

Heliocentric Thanks to Galileo, we now know that the Solar System is heliocentric. This means the Sun is at the center with the planets orbiting, or moving around, it.

The Sun is in the center

People used to think that the Earth was in the middle of the Solar System, and that the Sun and other planets moved around it. But another astronomer, Nicolaus Copernicus, thought the Sun was in the middle. When Galileo looked at the movement of the planets through a telescope, he found clues that proved Copernicus was right—the planets travel around the Sun.

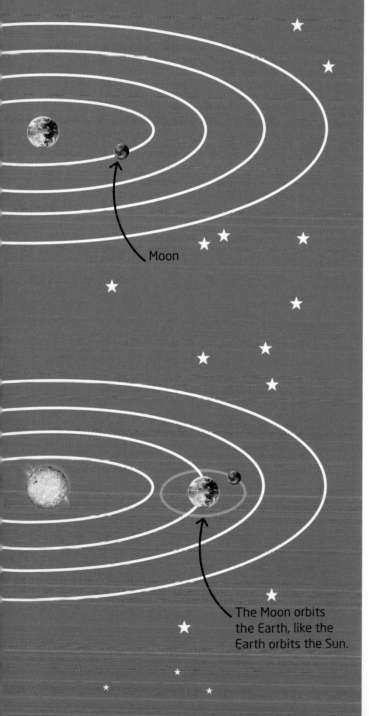

Moon

The Moon orbits the Earth, like the Earth orbits the Sun.

House arrest

The church in Galileo's time taught people that the Earth was at the center of the Solar System. They didn't like Galileo saying it wasn't, so they put him on trial and sentenced him to house arrest.

Galileo's **middle finger** is on display at a museum in **Florence, Italy.**

Printing press

Galileo may owe his success to the printing press, which was invented in the 15th century. It allowed lots of books to be printed quickly. Galileo used a telescope, which someone invented after playing with lenses. Lenses were popular because people needed glasses. And people needed glasses because so many people were reading!

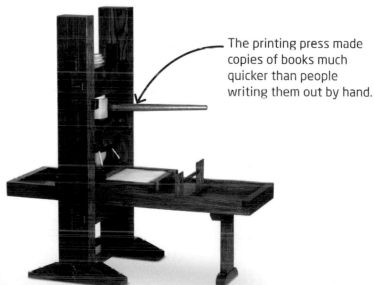

The printing press made copies of books much quicker than people writing them out by hand.

Make impact craters

Galileo was the first to realize that the Moon is covered in craters. We discovered how they got there when astronauts found signs of impacts by large space rocks. You can re-create these impacts at home.

Throw some marbles!

2

Drop marbles into the tray from above. Try using marbles of different sizes, and dropping them from different heights.

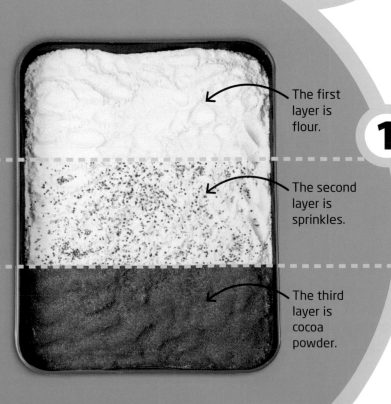

The first layer is flour.

1

The second layer is sprinkles.

Fill a tray with about an inch (a few centimeters) of flour. Cover the flour with colorful sprinkles, then use a sifter to sift a thin layer of cocoa powder over the top.

The third layer is cocoa powder.

What causes a crater?

Craters are caused by rocks flying in space. When one hits the Moon, a new crater is formed. There are craters on Earth, too, but we don't see as many craters on Earth as we do on the Moon. This is because craters on Earth get eroded, or worn away, by the Earth's weather. They can also slide under the Earth's surface after millions of years due to small shifts in the Earth's outer layer.

Meteor Crater in the Arizona desert

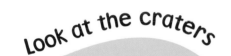

Look at the craters

These white lines are called rays.

Now try...

Try throwing the marbles into the tray at different speeds and angles. Do the shapes and sizes of the craters change?

3

Remove the marbles and look at the holes you've made—they are just like craters. You will see some scattered flour and sprinkles, too. This shows how rock from under the Moon's surface gets thrown out by the blast.

Raised crater rim

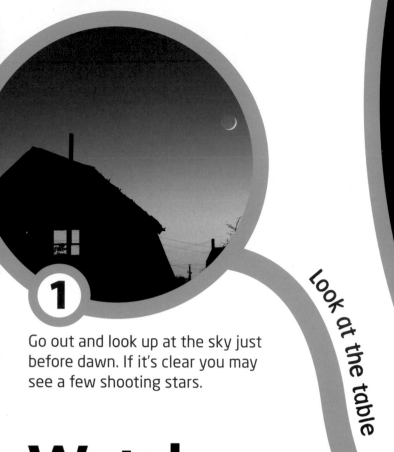

1

Go out and look up at the sky just before dawn. If it's clear you may see a few shooting stars.

Look at the table

Watch a meteor shower

Shooting stars aren't actually stars, they're rocks from space that burn up as they pass through the Earth's atmosphere. As the Earth goes around the Sun, it passes through areas with lots of rocks. At this time it's possible to see loads of shooting stars in what's called a meteor shower.

2

Check the table to the right for the best time of year to find a meteor shower in your area. If you're able to go outside to see one, draw or take notes of what you see.

Space rocks

Scientists call space rocks different things depending on where the rock is. A small rock in space is called a meteoroid. While a meteoroid is burning up in the Earth's atmosphere, it's called a meteor, or shooting star. If it doesn't burn up completely and actually reaches the Earth, it's called a meteorite.

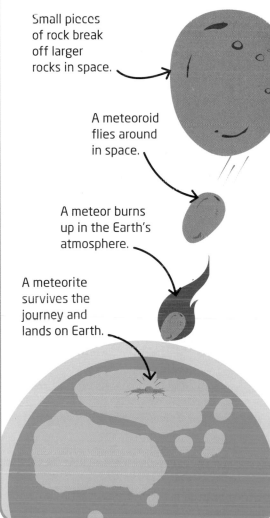

Small pieces of rock break off larger rocks in space.

A meteoroid flies around in space.

A meteor burns up in the Earth's atmosphere.

A meteorite survives the journey and lands on Earth.

What time is best?

This table tells you the best time to go looking for meteor showers in your part of the world.

Name of shower	Time of year	Where in the world
Lyrids	April 22-26	Northern hemisphere
Eta Aquarids	May 6	Southern hemisphere
Perseids	August 11-13	Both
Geminids	December 13-15	Both

Did you know?

Scientists find out lots of cool facts as they investigate the world around them. How many of these facts did you know?

Animal groups

Each of these six major animal groups has characteristics, or features, that make it different from the other groups. These groups make up most of the animals in the world.

Insects All insects have six legs and no backbone. There are more insects on Earth than any other type of animal.

Fish Fish live in water and breathe through slits in their body called gills. They lay eggs and use their fins to swim.

Reptiles These scaly, egg-laying animals live on land and are cold-blooded. Snakes, alligators, and turtles are all reptiles.

Amphibians Amphibians, such as frogs, toads, and salamanders, are cold-blooded. They can live both on land and in water.

Birds Birds lay eggs, are covered in feathers, and can usually fly. They are warm-blooded creatures.

Mammals Mammals, such as cheetahs and monkeys, are warm-blooded. They have skin covered in hair and feed their young milk. Humans are mammals!

Highest mountains in the world

Mount Everest At 29,029 ft (8,848 m), Mount Everest in Nepal is the tallest mountain in the world. More than 4,000 people have climbed to its top.

K2 K2 is located between China and Pakistan. It is 28,253 ft (8,611 m) tall. Many people agree K2 is the trickiest of these three mountains to climb.

Kanchenjunga Kanchenjunga is partly in India and partly in Nepal. It is 28,169 ft (8,586 m) high. Its name means "the five treasures of snow."

States of matter

Everything—whether it is alive, like an animal, or not alive, like a rock—is made of matter. The three states of matter are solid, liquid, and gas.

Solid The particles in solid matter are packed tightly together, so it has a definite shape. Melting a solid breaks the particles apart a bit, turning it into a liquid.

Liquid Liquid matter fits to the shape of its container because the particles are free to move around each other. Liquid becomes a solid when cooled and a gas when heated.

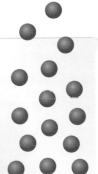

Gas The particles in gas are very spread out from one another, so gas can move around and rise out of a container. Nitrogen and carbon dioxide are gases found in the air.

Forces

Forces, like gravity and magnetism, push and pull on things. Simple forces can change an object's shape, or the speed or direction in which it's moving.

 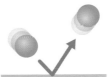 

Change shape
Pull on a slingshot to stretch it and change its shape.

Change direction
Bounce a ball to make it move in a different direction.

Change speed
Kick a ball hard to make it travel away fast.

Senses

Most people think humans only have the five senses shown below. But we actually have loads more than that, for example a sense of balance and a sense of temperature.

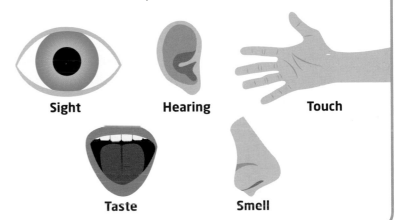

Sight   **Hearing**   **Touch**

Taste   **Smell**

The Earth and the Moon

All of the other planets in the Solar System could fit between the Earth and the Moon. It is a distance of 239,000 miles (384,400 km).

Glossary

adapt how a living thing changes its appearance or behavior to better fit in with its environment

apex predator animal at the top of its food chain that has no natural predators

atmosphere layer of gases that surrounds a planet

atom tiny building blocks that make up everything in the world

average one result that represents several results. It is found by adding all of the results together and dividing by the number of results

bacteria tiny creatures that can only be seen with a microscope

biomimicry when scientists and inventors look to nature for ideas

buoyancy upward force that makes an object float

chain reaction event where one action leads to the next, which leads to the next, and so on

chemical substance made when certain atoms stick together in a certain way

chemical reaction event in which atoms that were stuck together break apart and are rearranged into something new

circuit path through which electricity can flow in a continuous loop

decomposer creature that feeds on dead plants and animals, and returns nutrients into the soil

density how much matter there is in a certain amount of space. If two things take up the same amount of space, the denser one has more matter in it and is heavier

diffuse when one material spreads out into another, for example food dye spreading into water

dissolve when one substance is completely absorbed by another substance, for example salt dissolving in water

dome strong shape that engineers often include in buildings and bridges

drag force that works to slow down an object as it travels through a liquid or gas

electricity flow of electric charge that powers things

electron one of the three kinds of tiny particles inside an atom. Electricity is the flow of electrons

element particular type of atom

energy ability to do work, or to make something happen, either now or at some point in the future

Equator imaginary line that runs around the middle of the Earth, splitting it into northern and southern hemispheres

erosion changes in the surface of the Earth as features get worn away by the weather

ethologist scientist who studies animal behavior

evaporation liquid turning into a gas, such as hot water turning to steam

evolution process where a species changes, over many generations, to suit its environment

force push or pull that causes things to move, change direction, change speed, or stop moving

fossil plant or animal remains that have been preserved in rock over millions of years

fossil fuel type of natural fuel that burns easily, such as coal, natural gas, and oil

friction force that stops objects from sliding over each other

gravity force that pulls one object toward another and affects all objects in the Universe

habitat area where an animal or plant lives

hemisphere half of a planet, such as the northern and southern hemispheres of the Earth

kinetic energy energy something has when it is moving

lift force that pushes an object upward as it moves through the air

magma hot, semimelted rock that flows beneath the Earth's surface and erupts out of a volcano

magnetism force created by magnets, which pull some metals toward them

mass amount of matter in an object, which gives the object its weight

matter stuff that everything is made of

meteor small piece of space rock that burns up as it goes through the Earth's atmosphere

meteorite small rock from space that makes it through the Earth's atmosphere and lands on the Earth's surface

meteoroid small rock in space that has broken off from a bigger space rock

molecule group of atoms stuck together

mutation a new feature of an animal or a plant that doesn't come from a parent

nerves long strands connected to the brain that run through our bodies. They sense the world around us and control our muscles

nervous system collection of nerves inside the body through which the body sends signals to and from the brain

nuclear explosion huge burst of energy that occurs when atoms split in a chain reaction

nutrient substance that gives a living thing the energy or chemicals it needs to survive

orbit the path an object takes around another due to gravity, such as how planets travel around the Sun

organ body part that does a certain job, such as the heart or lungs

paleontologist scientist who studies fossils to learn about the history of life on Earth

parasite animal that lives on and feeds off another animal

periodic table a chart made by Dmitri Mendeleev that organizes all of the elements according to how they behave

photosynthesis process in which plants use energy from the Sun to make food

pollen powderlike plant substance that insects and other animals carry from one plant to another

polymer lots of atoms locked tightly together in a long chain

potential energy energy stored for later use, such as the energy in a slingshot elastic that has been pulled back, but not yet released

prism shaped glass or other see-through material that splits white light into a rainbow of colors

producer plant at the bottom of the food chain that makes its own food using energy from sunlight

radiation strong, invisible rays of energy, such as X-rays, that can be harmful over time

radioactivity ability of an object to give off radiation

sedimentary rock type of rock that forms from bits of earth being packed together over many, many years

sense how we know what the world is like. Human senses include sight, hearing, smell, taste, and touch

skeleton system of interlocking bones in the body that gives it structure

solar energy energy made from the Sun that can be used as an alternative to fossil fuels

soluble ability of one substance to be dissolved into another

stamen part of a flower that produces pollen

stigma sticky end of a flower that collects pollen from other flowers

surface tension force caused by tiny water particles sticking to each other, forming a kind of skin on the surface

tectonic plate one of the seven large, slowly moving chunks of the Earth's outermost layer

tensile strength how hard a material is to pull apart

thrust force that pushes an object, such as an airplane, forward through the air

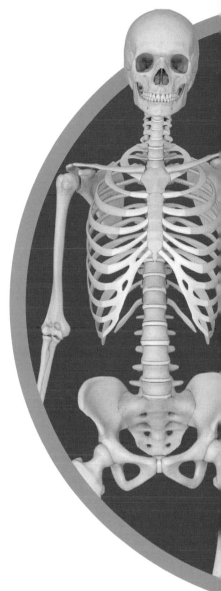

tornado dangerous column of quickly spinning air in contact with the ground

volcano opening in the outermost layer of the Earth through which hot liquid rock, called magma, can erupt

water cycle system of natural processes through which the Earth's water is recycled

X-ray type of radiation that can pass through most parts of the body and helps doctors to diagnose a patient's illness or injury

Index

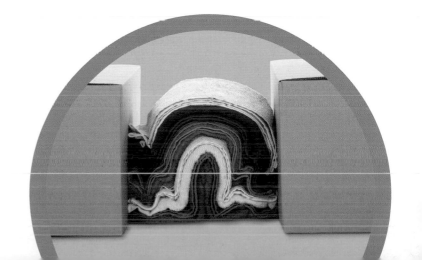

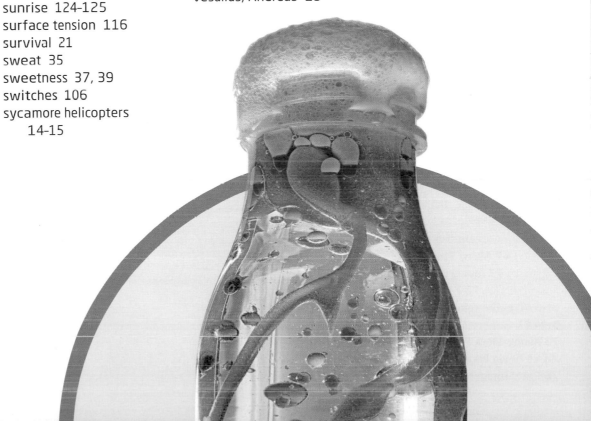